From Slave Cabin to the Pulpit: The Autobiography of Rev. Peter Randolph, and Sketches of Slave Life

Rev. Peter Randolph

FROM
SLAVE CABIN
TO
THE PULPIT.

THE AUTOBIOGRAPHY OF
REV. PETER RANDOLPH:

THE SOUTHERN QUESTION ILLUSTRATED
AND
SKETCHES OF SLAVE LIFE

1893

PREFACE.

IN giving the following sketches of my life to the public, I sincerely hope that literary defects, and errors of style, will be kindly overlooked. Though I have endeavored to improve myself, yet I cannot boast of an education, as my readers will doubtless see. These sketches of my life, since Emancipation, given in a simple style, illustrate, I think, some phases of the "Southern Question". They consist mainly of my own experience and observation in the South and North, as a slave and freeman.

With these biographical sketches, I have added for preservation, a pamphlet of sketches issued by me in 1855, on the "Peculiar Institution", with an introduction by Samuel May, Jr. This little work, which will be seen in the back part of the book, I desire to keep in print, for it has in it what I know to be truthful information on the subject of Slavery.

Slavery, we say, is dead; but the rising generations will ask: What was it?

To the children and descendants of that noble band of Anti-Slavery followers, and to the friends of humanity, I present these my experiences, in the name of God and Truth.

PETER RANDOLPH.

Boston, 1893.

CONTENTS.

I. EARLY LIFE

II. FREEDOM

III. IN BOSTON

IV. MY FRIENDS

V. CHURCH WORK

VI. IN A VIRGINIA PULPIT

VII. RELIGIOUS CONDITION

VIII. RELIGION AT THE CLOSE OF THE WAR

IX. A DISTINCTION

X. SPECIAL TRAITS

XI. IN MANY FIELDS

XII. THE LAW

XIII. RETROSPECT

XIV. SOME OF MY FRIENDS

SKETCHES OF SLAVE LIFE.

INTRODUCTORY NOTE

I. THE SYSTEM

II. SLAVES THE PLANTATION

III. FARMS ADJOINING EDLOE'S PLANTATION

IV. OVERSEERS

V. CUSTOMS OF THE SLAVES WHEN ONE OF THEIR NUMBER DIES

VI. SLAVES ON THE AUCTION BLOCK

VII. CITY AND TOWN SLAVES

VIII. RELIGIOUS INSTRUCTION

IX. SEVERING OF FAMILY TIES

X. COLORED DRIVERS

XI. MENTAL CAPACITY OF THE SLAVE .

XII. THE BLOOD OF THE SLAVE

CHAPTER I.

EARLY LIFE.

I WAS born a slave, and owned, with eighty- one others, by a man named Edloe, and among them all, only myself learned to either read or write. When I was a child, my mother used to tell me to look to Jesus, and that He who protected the widow and fatherless would take care of me also. At that time, my ideas of Jesus were the same as those of the other slaves. I thought he would talk with me, if I wished it, and give me what I asked for. Being very sickly, my greatest wish was to live with Christ in heaven, and so I used to go into the woods and lie upon my back, and pray that he would come and take me to himself—really expecting to see Him with my bodily eyes. I was then between ten and eleven years old, and I continued to look for Him until I began to feel very sorry that He would not come and talk with me; and then I felt that I was the worst. little boy that ever lived, and that was the reason Jesus would not talk to me. I felt so about it I wanted to die, and thought it would be just in God to kill me, and I prayed that he would kill me, for I did not want to live to sin against him any more. I felt so for many days an nights.

At last, I gave myself up to the Lord, to do what he would with me, for I was a great sinner. I began to see the offended justice of God. O, my readers, the anguish of my heart! I thought the whole world was on me, and I must die and be lost. In the midst of my troubles, I felt that if God would have mercy on me, I should never sin again. When I had come to this, I felt my guilt give way, and thought that I was a new being. Now, instead of looking with my real eyes to see my Saviour, I felt him in me, and I was happy. The eyes of my mind were open, and I saw things as I never did before. With my mind's eye, I could see my Redeemer hanging upon the cross for me.

I wanted all the other slaves to see him thus, and feel as happy as I did. I used to talk to others, and tell them of the friend they would have in Jesus, and show them by my experience how I was brought to Christ, and felt his love within my heart,— and love it was, in God's adapting himself to my capacity.

After receiving this revelation from the Lord, I became impressed that I was called of God to preach to the other slaves. I labored under this impression for seven years, but then I could not read the Bible, and I thought I could never preach unless I learned to read the Bible, but I had no one to teach me how to read. A friend showed me the letters, and how to spell words of three letters. Then I continued, until I got so as to read the Bible—the great book of God—the source of all knowledge. It was my great desire to read easily this book. I thought it was written by the Almighty himself. I loved this book, and prayed over it, and labored until I could read it. I used to go to the church to hear the white preacher. When I heard him read his text, I would read mine when I got home. This is the way, my readers, I learned to read the word of God when I was a slave. Thus did I labor eleven years under the impression that I was called to preach the gospel of Jesus Christ, the ever-blessed God.

Then I learned to write. Here I had no teaching; but I obtained a book with the writing alphabet in it, and copied the letters until I could write. I had no slate, so I used to write on the ground. All by myself I learned the art of writing. Then I used to do my own letter-writing, and write my own passes. When the slave wants to go from one plantation to another, he must have a pass from the overseer. I could do my own writing, unbeknown to the overseer, and carry my own pass.

My oldest brother's name was Benjamin. He was owned by C. H. Edloe, the same person who owned me. Benjamin was a very bright young man, and very active about his work. He was fond of laughing and frolicking with the young women on the plantation. This, Lacy the overseer, did not like, and therefore was always watching Benjamin, seeking an occasion to have him whipped. At one time, a pig had been found dead. The little pig could not tell why he was dead, and no one confessed a knowledge of his death; consequently, Lacy thought so great a calamity, so important a death, should be revenged. He advised Edloe to have every slave whipped. Edloe consented, expecting, probably, to prevent by such cruelty, any other pig from dying a natural death.

Lacy, the tender-hearted overseer, with a heart overflowing with sorrow at the great loss and sad bereavement of Edloe's plantation, took his rawhide, with a wire attached to the end of it, and gave each man twenty lashes on the bare back. O, monster! the blood was seen upon the side of the barn where these slaves were whipped for days and months. The wounds of these poor creatures prevented them from performing their daily tasks. They were, indeed, so cut up, that pieces came out of the backs of some of them, so that a child twelve or thirteen years old could lay his fist in the cruel place. My brother Benjamin was one of the slaves so savagely beaten.

One morning, Lacy—perhaps thinking piggy's death not wholly avenged—proposed again to whip my brother; but Benjamin did not agree with him as to the necessity of such proceedings, and determined not to submit; therefore, he turned his back upon Lacy, and his face to the woods, making all possible speed toward the latter. Lacy fired upon him, but only sent a few shot into his flesh, which did not in the least frighten Benjamin; it only served to make him run as fast as if he himself had been shot from the overseer's gun. For seven months, he lived in the swamps of Virginia, while every effort was made to catch him, but without success. He once ventured on board a vessel on the James River. There he was caught but soon made his escape again to the swamp, where my mother and myself used to carry him such food as we could procure to keep him alive. My poor broken-hearted mother was always weeping and praying about Benjamin, for the overseer had threatened that if he ever saw him, he would shoot him, as quick as he would a wild deer. All the other overseers had made the same threats.

Edloe, not thinking it best to take Benjamin on to his plantation (provided he could catch him), sold him to another man, who, after he had succeeded in his sham plan of buying my poor brother, sent for him to come out of the swamp and go with him. Benjamin went home to his new master, and went faithfully to work for him—smart young man that he was!

From Slave Cabin to the Pulpit

Sometimes Benjamin would steal over at night to see mother (a distance of ten miles). He could not come in the day-time, because Lacy still declared he would kill him the first time he saw him. He did see him one Sabbath, but having no gun or pistol with him, my brother again escaped him, thanks to the mercies of God. Benjamin continued to serve his new master, until he was suddenly bound and carried to Petersburg, Virginia, and sold to a negro-trader who put him in a slave-pen, until a large number of slaves were bought up by him, to be carried into bondage further South, there to lead miserable lives on the cotton and sugar plantations. Benjamin, my dear brother, left Petersburg, and I have not seen him since.

Thanks be unto God, prayer can ascend, and will be listened to by Him who answereth prayer! To him who crieth unto Him day and night, He will listen, and send His angel of peace to quiet his troubled heart, with the assurance that the down-trodden shall be lifted up, the oppressed shall be delivered from his oppressor, all captives set free, and all oppressors destroyed, as in ancient times. I know that God heard the prayers of my praying mother, because she was a Christain, and a widow, such as feared God and loved his commandments. She used often to sing the following hymn—

"Our days began with trouble here,
Our lives are but a span,

White cruel death is always near—
What a feeble thing is man!

Then sow the seed of grace while young,
That when you come to die,
You may sing the triumphant song,
Death! where's thy victory ?"

With the above lines has my mother often soothed, for a time, her own sorrows, when she thought of her poor son, so far away from her, she knew not where, neither could she know of his sufferings; and again, she would become a prey to bitter grief. Her only hope was to meet her son in heaven, where slaveholders could not come with their purchase-money, where Lacy could not come with his dogs, his guns, or his pistols, with powder or balls; neither would she have to steal away to see him, with a little food well concealed. Neither will Benjamin be obliged to crouch in the forest, hearing the midnight cry of wild beasts around him, while he seeks repose upon the cold, bare ground. No, she will meet him at the right hand of the Redeemer, who will wipe the briny tears from the eyes of the poor slave, and feed him with the hidden treasures of His love.

MY PARENTS.

My father did not belong to Edloe, but was owned by a Mr. George Harrison, whose plantation adjoined that of my master. Harrison made my father a slave-driver, placing an overseer over him. He was allowed to visit my mother every Wednesday and every Saturday night. This was the time usually given to the slaves to see their wives. My father would often tell my mother how the white overseer had made him cruelly whip his fellows, until the blood ran down to the ground. All his days, he had to follow this dreadful employment of flogging men, women and children, being placed in this helpless condition by the tyranny of his master. I used to think very hard of my father, and that he was a very cruel man; but when I knew that he could not help himself, I could not but alter my views and feelings in regard to his conduct. I was ten years old when he died.

When my father died, he left my mother with five children. We were all young at the time, and mother had no one to help take care of us. Her lot was very hard indeed. She had to work all the day for her owner, and at night for those who were dearer to her than life; for what was allowed her by Edloe was not sufficient for our wants. She used to get a little corn, without his knowledge, and boil it for us to satisfy our hunger. As for clothing, Edloe would give us a coarse suit once in three years; mother sometimes would beg the cast-off garments from the neighbors, to cover our nakedness; and when they had none to give, she would sit and cry over us, and pray to the God of the widow and fatherless for help and succor. At last, my oldest brother was sold from her, and carried where she never saw him again. She went mourning for him all her days, like a bird robbed of her young—like Rachel bereft of her children, who would not be comforted, because they were not. She departed this life on the 27th of September, 1847, for that world "where the wicked cease from troubling, and the weary are at rest."

CHAPTER II.

FREEDOM.

My Master! Carter H. Edloe made his will six years before his decease. He said to some of his slaves, just before his death, that he had another will, which he had given into the bands of a lawyer in Petersburg, Va., to keep for him, but this will was never heard from. The slaves knew about it, but their voice or testimony was nothing; therefore, nothing could be done about it.

I present that will here, together with the decree of the Court respecting it, in order that my readers may judge for themselves as to the intention of our master, and be convinced that what I have to say in reference to the manner in which the will was executed is perfectly just, and warranted by the facts.

IN THE NAME OF GOD, AMEN!—I, CARTER H. EDLOE, of the County of Prince George, being of sound mind and disposing memory, but considering the uncertainty of life, do make and ordain this to be my last Will and Testament:

1st. I desire that all debts that I may owe at the time of my decease, shall be paid out of the money on hand or the profits of my estate.

2nd. I desire that my estate shall be kept together and cultivated to the best advantage, until a sufficient sum can be raised to pay my debts, should there be any deficiency in the amount of money on hand and debts due to me, and to raise a sufficient sum to pay for the transportation of my Slaves to any Free State or Colony which they may prefer, and give to each Slave Fifty Dollars on their departure, either in money or other articles which may suit them better; but should any of my slaves prefer going immediately, they can do so, but they are not to be furnished with money. It is not my wish to force them away without their consent, In the event of any of them preferring to remain in slavery, they must take the disposition hereinafter directed.

3d. After the provisions in the preceding clauses of my Will have been complied with, I loan to my niece, Elizabeth C. Orgain, my plantation in Prince George, called Mt. Pleasant, during her life, but in the event of her marrying and having children, I then give to her children, at her death, the said land, to them and their heirs forever.

4th. I loan to my niece, Mary Orgain, my Plantation in Prince George, called Brandon and Dandridge's, during her life; but should she marry and have children, I then give to her children, at her death, the said lands, to them and their heirs forever.

5th. The rest and residue of my estate, of whatever kind soever, I desire may be divided into two equal parts, and one part to go to each of my nieces, Elizabeth and Mary; and should any of my slaves prefer remaining in slavery, I desire they may be divided into two equal parts, and one part go to each of my nieces, during their lives, and then to their children, in the same manner as the landed property is given, except my Household Furniture, Wines and Liquors, all of which I give to Mary Orgain during her life and then to her children. Those negroes under age at my death may have until they are twenty-one years of age to decide whether they will go or remain; but in the event of but one of my nieces having children, I desire that those children have the whole of my property at the death of their aunt.

6th. I give and bequeath to my female slave, Harriet Barber, and her children (all of whom I bought of R. G. Orgain, Esq.), Eight Thousand Dollars, which sum I desire my Executors to take from my estate, and either lay it out in good stock, or put the money out at interest, always taking undoubted security—the stock I should prefer—the interest of which shall be paid to said Harriet yearly. Should there not be a sum sufficient to pay this legacy, either in stock or money, I direct my Executors to sell my land in Southampton. Should that not make up the deficiency, other land must be sold, or horses and cattle, as my Executors may think best.

7th. It is my wish that the said Harriet and children should remain on my estate, or in any situation which they may prefer that the law will allow; and I direct my Executors to furnish Harriet and her children with their Free Papers, whenever they may desire to have them, and assist them to remove to any place they may choose to locate themselves.

I do hereby appoint David D. Brydon, of the Town of Petersburg, and John A. Seldon, of Charles City County, my Executors, requiring them to give no security for the performance of their duty. I do hereby revoke all former Wills, this being my last Will. In testimony whereof, I have hereunto subscribed my name, this 20th day of March, One Thousand Eight Hundred and Thirty-Eight.

CARTER H. EDLOE.

At a Court of Quarterly Sessions, held for Prince George County, at the Court House thereof, on Tuesday, the 13th day of August, 1844:

This last Will and Testament of *Carter H. Edloe*, dec'd, was presented into Court, and there being no subscribing witnesses thereto, William C. Rawlings, P. C. Osborne, and David Tennant, appeared in Court and made oath that they are well acquainted with the handwriting of the Testator, and they verily believe the said Will to be wholly written by the Testator: And thereupon said Will is ordered to be recorded. On the motion of John A. Seldon, an Executor therein named, who made oath thereto, and entered into and acknowledged a bond in the penalty of One Hundred and Twenty Thousand Dollars (the Testator desiring that no security should be given upon his qualification), conditioned as the law directs, certificate is granted the said John A. Seldon for obtaining a probate of the said Will in due form.

Teste,

RO. GILLIAM, *Clerk.*

VIRGINIA—*Prince George County, to wit:*

I, ROBERT GILLIAM, Clerk of the Court of said county, in the State of' Virginia, do hereby certify the foregoing to be a true copy of the last Will and Testament of Carter H. Edloe, deceased.

In testimony whereof, I have hereto set my hand and affixed the seal of the said [SEAL.] Court, this thirty-first day of August, 1847, and in the seventy-second year of the Commonwealth.

RO. GILLIAM, *Clerk.*

DECREE OF THE COURT.

VIRGINIA:

At a Circuit Superior Court of Law and Chancery, held for the town of Petersburg, at the court house thereof, on Monday, the 24th day of May, A. D. 1847:

John A. Seldon, Executor of C. H. Edloe, deceased, Plaintiff,

against

Mary Orgain and Elizabeth Orgain, infants, by H. B. Gaines, their Guardian *ad litem,* &c., Defts.,

In Chancery.

This cause came on this day to be further heard on the papers formerly read, on the reports of Commissioner Bernard, and of the special Commissioners appointed to consult the slaves of C. H. Edloe, deceased, and was argued by counsel: *On consideration whereof,* the court being of opinion that the slave Harriet and her children are entitled to no part of the profits of the plantation, and that the several sums charged in the account of profits as expended for them ought not to have been so charged; and adopting the correction of the report in that particular, contained in the note of the Commissioner, p. 1., doth order that the report of Commissioner Bernard, with that correction, and the report of the special

Commissioners, be confirmed: And the court doth further adjudge, order and decree, that the Plaintiff do, on or before the fifteenth day of October, one thousand eight hundred and forty-seven, as may seem to him best, discharge from servitude all the slaves of his Testator; that he deliver to said slaves, individually or in families, as he may think best, duly authenticated copies of this decree, endorsing on each copy the name or names of the person or persons to whom it is given; that the Executor, out of the money now in his hands and interest thereon from the thirteenth day of March, one thousand eight hundred and forty-seven, together with the nett proceeds of the growing crop or such thereof as may be secured, pay to the slaves, Robert, Old Ben and Caty (who elect to remain in service until the full amount of the provision intended for them shall be raised), each the sum of Fifty Dollars, "on their departure"; that he pay to each of the slaves of the Testator who has remained on the plantation, and shall so remain until the slaves shall be liberated as herein directed, a sum sufficient to pay for his or her transportation to such free State or colony as they may respectively prefer, or provide and pay for their transportation to such free State or colony in such other manner as may to him seem best: And the court doth order that the said Executor do immediately, on discharging the said slaves from servitude, cause them to be removed to the free State or colony which they may respectively select as their future homes; the court being of opinion that it was not the intention of the Testator that they should be emancipated and allowed to receive the bounty provided for them, unless they were removed by the Executor beyond the limits of Virginia; and in case the fund be not sufficient to defray the whole amount of such expenses of transportation, the same shall be divided among the slaves, rateably, taking into consideration their ages, place selected, &c., and that he distribute the residue, if any there be, equally among all the said slaves, without regard to age, and that he deliver the slaves Sylvia and Jenny, who elect to remain slaves, to the defendants, to whom they are bequeathed by the Will of the Testator.

And it is further ordered, that the Plaintiff settle before a Commissioner a further account of his transactions as Executor, which account the Commissioner is directed to report to the court, with any matter specially stated deemed pertinent by himself, or which any of the parties may require to be so stated.

A copy—Teste,

                                      R. McMANN, S. C.

AUGUST 6th, 1847.

When Edloe died, he gave this will, which was the one finally acted upon, into the hands of one of his slaves, not feeling willing to trust any one else.

The Executor of the estate was John A. Seldon, of Charles City County. The will stated, as will be seen, that if there should be any deficiency of money on hand, sufficient must be raised to pay his debts, and transport his slaves to a place of freedom, and pay each of them fifty dollars. Edloe was gone, and could not act for us in person, so this deed of justice was not carried out. Mr. Seldon interpreted the will thus: We were to stay on the plantation and work there till we had earned this money ourselves, and then we were to be free. Meantime, he took from us what the overseer had hitherto given us, and took our earnings, too.

For six months, all knowledge of this will was kept from us. I was the only one among the slaves who could read and write. This I had kept secret, for fear of the consequences. A friend, who seemed very much interested in our affairs, showed me a copy of this will, upon promise of secrecy. So I read it, and remembered it all; then he told me of a lawyer who would be a good one for us. I communicated this good news to two of the older and more experienced men of our party, and repeated to them the substance of the will. They went to see the lawyer, and he agreed to take the case in hand. This friend knew how we were treated, and told us it was very unjust and wrong. This lawyer's name was James L. Scarborough, of Prince George County, Va.

From Slave Cabin to the Pulpit

He first went to the bank of Petersburg, where Edloe's money was deposited, and found out that there were thirty-two thousand dollars on hand; so he was going at once to get our free papers for us; but soon he came to us again, and said the executor of the estate would give him five hundred dollars to stop the suit—but he would not stop it. But this did not last long. We soon found that Seldon got all our money, and could give him more than we could; so he began to put us off from one court to another, telling us that the court did not have time to attend to us, but the next would certainly settle the matter. We gave him all our little earnings, which amounted to twenty-two dollars, but he got no papers. So he kept us for two years and six months. When we found out the deception he had practiced upon us, we felt very wretched indeed—sure that we had no friend left, and should never get our freedom, but were cruelly robbed of what was our own, not only by right, but as an especial gift.

Seldon used to come and see us when the crops were to be sold, get the money for us (but we never saw it), then go away again, without the least advantage to us. At last, we took courage, and got another man to exert himself for us. He was not a *lawyer*, but a magistrate. His name was William B. Harrison, the owner of middle Brandon. Though a slaveholder himself, he got our free papers, and procured us a passage to Boston, after we had remained three years and thirty-five days in unlawful bondage, according to the laws of Virginia, to say nothing of a higher law.

Instead of the fifty dollars we were each to receive on our landing, we had fourteen dollars and ninety-six cents apiece. All our money was taken from us, because we were black people; but glad enough were we of our freedom.

We were told if we came to Boston, we should be killed, or put in prison, where we should have to work under ground or be obliged to drag carts all round the streets; but we were determined to try it, live or die.

We came in 1847, and have not been eaten up yet. And now we claim the fifty dollars, and interest, since 1844. It was given to us by the man we served while he was living, and no law or justice can keep it from us, except by downright fraud. Here are old people of the party unable to do much for themselves, to whom this would be a great blessing. Surely, the day is not far distant when those base men will be shown up to the world for what they are worth. The wrong they committed will not rest upon those ignorant slaves, but will rebound back, covering their white faces, but black hearts, with infamy.

CHAPTER III.

IN BOSTON.

I CAME to Boston on the 15th of September, 1847, in company with sixty-six men, women and children, who were emancipated by the will of Carter H. Edloe, the owner of a large farm in Prince George County, Virginia, known as the Brandon Plantation, as my readers will see from the copy of the will.

In order to gain the freedom given us by the provision of the will, it was necessary that we should leave the South, and seek a new home in the North. Consequently, on the 5th of September, we left our homes, embarked on the ship known as the "Thomas H. Thompson," in charge of Captain Wickson, and arrived at Boston, as stated above.

It was soon noised abroad through the city, that a cargo of emancipated slaves had landed at Long Wharf. A large number of citizens came to the wharf to see the strangers, and to congratulate them on their new birth to freedom. Prominent among these were, William Loyd Garrison, John A. Andrew, Wendell Phillips, and Samuel May. These noble and patriotic men, who lived in the trying times of the country's history, have all passed away from the active scenes of life, and there are but few left, who lived in their times, to tell the story of their deeds.

Need I say, we were made welcome to our new home, when we met such distinguished visitors. The kindness and charity shown were more than we expected. Permit me to say here, that John A. Andrew, who was afterward elected governor of Massachusetts, was one of my warmest personal friends, and remained so until his death. As I became acquainted with him he seemed to take great delight in talking with me relative to my former condition, and that of my companions. He was anxious to hear the story of my religious conversion, and how I learned to read and write. He became so familiar with my spiritual convictions, and views of faith, that in his last lecture delivered in Music Hall, Boston, while alluding to the subject of faith, he made the remark that my definition of faith was one of the best he had ever heard.

Many friends who heard the lecture, afterward spoke to me concerning my definition of faith as I had related it to Governor Andrew. I speak of this, simply to show the noble spirit of the man toward the unfortunate. I, born an ignorant slave, he, an educated lawyer, yet he did not disdain to talk with me on the great subject of religion.

After we had been visited by the distinguished friends that I have mentioned, we left the vessel and the wharf, and found ourselves promenading up the free streets of Boston.

You may imagine our curiosity and elation as we were introduced and looked upon the new scenes that were about us. Truly we were in a new world. Think of three score and more souls, blind as bats—so far as the letter is concerned; for I was the only one who could read or write—coming fresh, and directly from a Southern plantation, empty-handed and ignorant of their environments, and you will have some idea of myself and company as we made our advent in Boston.

I will state here, if I have not elsewhere, that on leaving Virginia, the lawyer, William Joins, who was interested in us, gave us a letter of introduction to William Loyd Garrison, the true friend of the poor slave. On leaving the vessel some of us went to the office of Mr. Garrison, which at that time was located at 21 Cornhill, Boston. Here we met other strong antislavery friends, whose glad welcome and warm grasp of the hand—I imagine I can feel it now—convinced us beyond a doubt that we were among our friends.

Mr. Garrison and Rev. Samuel May, with others of the Antislavery Party, were active in securing situations for us. About half of our number, without much loss of time, found places out of the city, and the remainder in and about the city.

Thus distributed, we had to work out our own destiny with all the disabilities that the peculiar institution had entailed upon us. Now, we had to prove to the world, whether or not, the oft-repeated assertion was true, "That the slave, if emancipated, could not take care of himself."

Of course, in our struggles, many of us felt sorely the need of an education in the midst of the new surroundings. Many of the old ones passed away from earth without realizing this coveted possession. Though they were destitute of a practical education, yet they were not ignorant of a personal knowledge of Christ.

Permit me to return again and speak more definitely concerning myself. As I have already intimated, I repeat, by saying, that the little education I possessed gave me some advantages that were out of the reach of my companions. Knowing how to read and write was of no little value to me, for it made me more in demand, and assisted me in discharging more effectually the duties I had to perform by those who employed me.

My chief difficulty was not in getting much work, but in getting much pay—I had much work but little pay. I received a dollar and a half per week with board, until I was employed at the fair given by the members of the Anti-Slavery Society, in December, 1847.

At this fair I had the opportunity of meeting a number of noble-hearted men and women, who stood ready to help me in various ways. Also, I listened attentively to the lectures and discussions given under the auspices of this society. The language and words used by some, in describing and denouncing the slave power, were strong and uncompromising, yet the words were inadequate and too weak to express the barbarity and cruelty to which my brethren in the South were exposed.

As I listened and conversed with these earnest men, I was impressed, also, with the idea that they were not familiar with all the relations that existed between the master and slave, though they were well posted on the subject.

Another thing impressed me relative to these debates, and that was, that there were honest men in Boston—and some of them my friends—who were in favor of slavery. They seemed to argue from a property point of view; they said that the slaves were the property of the owners, and that the masters as a matter of fact, would not destroy that which they regarded as their legitimate property.

At a glance this would seem to be a plausible argument, but one familiar with the system as I am could not take that view. I saw at once what was the difficulty: the thing needed was more definite knowledge in regard to the masters and their slaves. This I felt I could supply from my experience in the South as a slave. Accordingly, I was prevailed upon to write and publish the little work, entitled, "The Sketch of a Slave life, or, an illustration of the peculiar institution."

In this work I tried to set forth as best I could, in plain and simple language, the true relation that existed between the slave and his owner. Especially did I emphasize the point which seemed to trouble many of my pro-slavery friends. I endeavored to show that much of the cruel treatment inflicted on the slaves did not come directly from the masters, but from the slave-drivers or overseers, who for the time being had unlimited control.

No one will doubt, that some of the masters were inclined to be humane and have compassion on their slaves, if not from the promptings of humanity, certainly from the property considerations. But even if the master was kind, the overseers, whom the law protected, and from whom there was no appeal on the part of the slave, could maltreat and abuse with impunity. The laws that governed and controlled the inhuman institution were wrong and were the result of a depraved human nature. The time will come when the great Judge of the earth will judge between the oppressed and the oppressor.

CHAPTER IV.

MY FRIENDS.

IN this chapter I desire to mention some of the business men and firms that gave me employment during my earlier struggles in Boston. And it goes without saying, that the business community to-day in Boston, is not the business community of forty-five or fifty years ago, when I came to the city. Many of the names I shall mention have closed their final accounts on this earth and have gone to join the silent majority.

If some of the prominent merchants of forty years ago could be permitted to return again to the active scenes of their commercial life, and behold the mammoth and towering business blocks, cars flying through the streets without horses, and see their old aristocratic homes turned into dry-goods houses, I imagine they would ask some stranger, "What city is this."

I am pleased to say, there are still living children and grandchildren of many of these old families, who have been kind and thoughtful to me, because of my long and intimate acquaintance with their parents. I feel that I owe them a debt of gratitude, because in the midst of these radical changes, they have not forgotten their fathers or the principles which they espoused.

I do not think it improper or out of taste for me to mention some of these my early and life-long friends.

There was the well-known firm of Joseph Dix & Brown, the junior partner of which was Mr. J. C. Elms, who is now the honored president of the Shoe and Leather Bank, of Boston. I would also mention the firms of Isaac Fenno, Michal Simpson, of the Sackville Carpet Co., William Bond & Son, Mr. T. C. Marian, the firm of Little & Brown, the Boston Transcript, then in charge of Messrs. Henry W. Dutton and Daniel Haskill, the well-known merchant, Mr. Henry Callender, Mr. Morey, and the house of Merrett & Mullen, Mr. Tiler

Batcheller, of the firm of E.T. Batcheller & Co., shoe manufacturers, Mr. Chas. Adams, William B. Spooner, and Ezekias Chase.

These are some of the firms and business men I worked for years ago. Most of these had implicit confidence in me, and usually trusted me with their keys.

Many pleasant anecdotes might be related in connection with some of these. And here I will return and speak of a few in detail.

During my engagement with Mr. C. Marian, I must say, I knew little or nothing about how business should be conducted, I was as green as a cucumber, but was instructed by one of the clerks, Mr. Baker, to make a deposit at the bank. On entering the bank I handed over to the Cashier the money and book, who took the same, and said that it was all right, and kept the book. I was much perplexed and excited because he had taken the money and did not return the book. In my perplexed condition I hastened back to the office and began to relate my story, how the bank man had possession of the money and book, and refused to return the book of deposit. I thought sure the cashier had taken advantage of me.

When Mr. Baker and the other clerks saw my earnestness and excited condition about the matter they began to laugh, and rather enjoyed it at my expense, but Mr. Baker explained to me afterward that he forgot to tell me, that it was time for the book to be posted, and the cashier kept it for that purpose. These gentlemen have stepped off the stage of action, but their memory to me is frought with nothing but kindness.

While employed with the firm of Little & Brown, the latter manifested his interest in me by securing for me the janitorship of Harvard College buildings. He urged me to take the situation, but I refused, because I did not feel myself competent to assume such a place and responsibility.

From Slave Cabin to the Pulpit

Years after I left the Transcript office, Mr. Henry Dutton, or some of the family, would always remind me of Thanksgiving, by seeing to it that I had the typical New England dinner—"turkey with fixings."

Mr. Daniel Haskill, of the Transcript, was a great help to me in getting my little book —"Sketches of Slave Life"—before the public. He gave publicity to it through the columns of his paper, and said in his editorial, that he "had seen more in the little pamphlet, than he had read in volumes on the subject of slavery." From this announcement there was a great demand for my little book, and I was compelled to issue a second edition.

Mr. Henry Callender, of whom I spoke, and whose family has remained among my warmest friends, was also much help to me in my work at Richmond, Va., among the freedmen, at the close of the war; of which I shall speak later.

The way in which I got acquainted with Mr. Frank Merrett, of the firm of Merrett & Mullen, was a little singular. He wanted a man to work for him, and Mr. W. B. Morey, with whom I was engaged, recommended me. We talked the matter over, and came to an agreement. Finally, he remarked, that as he did not know me, he wished me to come to his house every morning and get the keys. This gave me the impression that he did not want to trust me with the keys over night. And I said to him, "Sir, I try to act on the square with all mankind." He looked sharply at me, and said, "Are you a mason?" I answered in the affirmative. He said nothing more, but gave me the keys to carry day and night.

I gave a lecture in one of the colored churches, on "the Misery and Folly of Idleness." Mr. Merrett made it convenient to come and hear me. Afterward, whenever in his store he saw a place where the feather-duster did not reach, or a stray cobweb about, he would remind me of that lecture, intimating that I should practice what I preached. Mr. Merrett was thoughtful and kind to me. And though a Universalist, he was a true friend to the poor and the oppressed.

During my stay with Mr. Tiler Batcheller, Mr. Charles Adams, whom I have already mentioned in the list of my friends, asked me to wash up his floor. He inquired how much I wanted for the same.

I told him I wanted three dollars a day. "Why!" said he, "Deacon (for that was the name they called me), "that is as much as they get in the legislature." Again I reminded him that my work was worth more. Mr. Adams was a member of the legislature and often joked me, because I said that I was worth more per day scrubbing floors, than he was in making laws for the state of Massachusetts. He was afterward elected State treasurer, but continued my warm friend. Oh, how happily I recall those good old times, of friendship and good will.

Among my list of friends I must not forget to mention Messrs. Fredrick and George Batcheller, who took much interest in me and always stood ready to help me.

At the memorial meeting held by the merchants of Boston, in honor of Mr. Geo. Batcheller, I was one of the number that was to make an address. Of course most of the gentlemen assembled were merchants, prominent and successful. I, though a colored man, with humble occupation and the only one among them, felt and sympathized with them on account of the loss of a valuable friend.

Those who spoke had their notes with them. And doubtless I may have had some of that feeling that accompanies a strange cat in a strange garret, but I was there to speak just as I felt. When I arose to speak without notes my friends exhibited no little anxiety, for they thought I would fail. At the close of the exercises, however, I was highly congratulated. A day or two afterward, a reporter of a New York paper, who was present, came and asked for my written address, as he had others. I informed him that I had none, and that he would have to write what he remembered. In the New York paper he reported a good analysis of my address.

What old resident of Boston does not remember William B. Spooner, the great temperance advocate. He was among my earliest friends, and I cannot close this chapter without giving him a passing comment. He was a man ready to talk with me on all subjects, secular and religious. Though he was a Unitarian, and I a Baptist, yet we agreed on many important points, because we both thought man ought to be good. On one occasion, in the course of our conversation, I made the remark that ever since I came out of slavery, I had been trying to make a man of myself.

As I was passing his office one day, he called me into his counting room, and said —

"Randolph, you told me something a year or two ago that I have been thinking about." He kept me in suspense for a little while, for, as we had talked over many things, I could not recall what it was. Finally, he said, "You told me some time ago that you had tried to make a man of yourself ever since you had left slavery. I think," said he, "you have succeeded very well."

Mr. Spooner was a great help to me in my work among the colored people in the South, at the close of the war. He made a visit in that section, and on his return North, gave a good account of my work.

In this connection, I do not want to forget my old friend, Mr. Nathaniel Conner, of the firm of N. Jones & Company. He belongs in the first rank with many others of my warm friends.

The last but not least of those of whom I now speak in detail, is Deacon Ezekias Chase, well known in Boston for his generous spirit and Christian principles. I will return and speak of him in connection with my church work in Boston.

CHAPTER V.
CHURCH WORK.

AMONG the first things I did after arriving in Boston, was that of looking after my church connection. In Virginia, I was a member of the Baptist Church. And naturally enough on coming here I sought to identify myself with that society.

I found a body of brethren worshiping in a hall on Belknap Street, now Joy Street. They were about fifteen in number, and were being supplied by Leonard A. Grimes. Myself and most of my companions who were professing Christians, joined this small body. Soon after, a council was called and our society was regularly organized and called the Twelfth Baptist Church. Rev. Mr. Grimes was properly ordained, and called to the pastorate of the new church. The history of this church and its distinguished pastor is well known to the older citizens of Boston, because of the prominence of both church and pastor in the early anti-slavery struggles.

I feel sad when I stop to recount, that I am the only living surviver of that original body.

I was licensed as a Baptist preacher by the above-named church, and continued my membership with them; but went out working for, and laboring with, other churches and telling the story of my bond-brethren in the South. I felt that God had called me from slavery to freedom, and from spiritual darkness to soul liberty, for a purpose, and that a part of my work was to remember and help those in bonds as if bound with them.

In 1852, I visited St. John, New Brunswick, as a missionary, for the purpose of preaching and helping the colored people in that vicinity who had gone from the States. About this time the fugitive slave law was in operation. This law was a terror, and brought untold suffering to the colored people, especially those who had escaped from slavery. Many were pursued, hounded down, and carried back into slavery. During this reign of terror, not a few colored people left the States and sought protection under the British Crown, in Canada.

While in St. John and vicinity I visited Lake Loma, a colored settlement. This was a colony that had been settled and fostered under the auspices of the Queen. During the war of 1812, between England and the United States, slaves from the South made their escape under British protection, and many of them were quartered at this place. At the time I visited them, I found that they had made little or no progress from an educational point of view, though they had been there fifty years.

This was probably due to the fact that prior to this time they had had no schools. After this schools were furnished them by the British Government, and the improved development was clearly seen.

I will here relate a little incident that will illustrate their megre surroundings. Arrangements were made that I should preach for them three times on the Sabbath, but I was urged to stay and preach on Monday morning, also. I consented providing the service would close in time to allow me to catch the ten o'clock stage. This was the mail stage, and the only public conveyance for travelling, coming twice a week. Providence seemed to order it otherwise than I intended. For just as I had commenced my sermon, along came the stage about nine o'clock. Of course I gave up the idea of leaving then, and continued through the whole service. It was a magnificent sight to see such a large congregation out on Monday morning to divine service, just as though it was Sunday. They seemed to enjoy my visit and sermons, and many outward manifestations were given showing the favorable impressions. Naturally enough, after the service, I was a little anxious about how I should get back to St. John, a distance of seventeen miles.

The brethren were not slow in coming to my assistance in this matter, though I must admit the conveyance was a slow one, namely, an ox-team. Now, the ox is a valuable animal and distinguished for his strength, but he is not to be counted on for rapidity, especially in catching a train. This was doubtless the best they had, and I accepted and marched on. After they had carried me a part of the journey, I decided that I could travel faster than the oxen. Accordingly, I put my feet in the path, and arrived at St. John about six P. M. I was hungry as a tramp, and needed no persuasion to eat.

I was disappointed in my visit to St. John, therefore my work there was not very satisfactory to me. I had always cherished the idea that when I stood on British soil, I should leave behind me the miserable race prejudice and hate. But to my surprise I found this state of things as bad in Canada, as in the States, and it may have appeared to me worse, because I was not looking for it. The word "negger", with taunting insults, seemed to meet me at every turn. The boys and young men would sing out, "Hello, negger. There's a negger from the States," and other such epithets. I noticed that the class that was always ready to hurl at me these insults wore worse clothes than I did. This was a source of gratification to me. And besides, I had heard so much about the excellent people in the British Provinces that I came dressed in my best, to the credit of the good people.

I must say, that it was not the better class that insulted me, but the worst, for I found in this vicinity many of the best of people, who were sympathetic, and were true friends of the colored race, but the diabolical system of slavery had made its influence felt even in the British territory, and there were those who were ready to look upon the colored man only as a bondman.

After my short missionary tour to St. John and vicinity, I took the boat for Boston. On my arrival I was taken suddenly ill, and confined to my bed for three weeks. But finally I was restored to health and went on with my work.

While speaking of my religious work and experience, I will also note a few habits and customs of the times, in connection with the same.

In these times of which I speak it was not customary for a colored preacher to address a white congregation; various were the views maintained by the white people relative to the colored man. Some said that he was not a member of the human family; others, that he was void of a moral and intellectual nature.

A large number thought he had little or no right to speak in a religious meeting. Here is a simple illustration of the point in view. I was invited by a brother minister to preach for his congregation, which was then worshiping in Milk Row, Somerville, Mass., in a hall. I reluctantly accepted the invitation, and on the Sunday and hour arranged put in my appearance.

One of the congregation, a teamster by occupation, when he saw me enter inquired of the pastor who was going to preach. He remarked that Rev. Peter Randolph, a colored preacher from Boston, would occupy the pulpit. The aforesaid gentleman felt insulted, took his hat and departed, saying that he did not care to hear that "negger" preach.

After the introductory services were over I had taken my text, and was about entering upon my discourse when in came my offended brother, and took a seat where he could look me right in the face. My text was, "Behold, old things are passed away and all are become new"—my theme being the new birth. At the close of the services he was asked how he liked the sermon. His answer was, that he was happily disappointed. It was quite evident that this man, full of prejudice, could not tell how far a toad could hop, by looking at his size.

I preached also in the afternoon, and this same brother was present and seemed to enjoy the sermon as well as anyone. My text was taken from Nehemiah—"I am doing a great work and cannot come down." I tried to show the disadvantages under which the children of Israel labored in rebuilding the walls of Jerusalem, and how important it was for them to stick to the work. I did not then know the condition of the society I was addressing, but was afterward informed that they were on the eve of disbanding. I also learned that they were much encouraged by what I had to say to them, and they resolved to continue together. The church became one of the largest in Somerville. I simply speak of this to show the wonder-working power of God. His ways are not our ways. They are past finding out. Man says, can any good thing come out of Nazareth, but God brings it out, and takes the weak and foolish things to confound the great. He is no respecter of persons, but a discerner of the heart and purposes of men.

In Dorchester, where I was invited to preach, I had a similar experience to that at Somerville—a strong objection to hearing the "negger preacher". This may be added also that the objector did finally hear me, and it is the last sermon he heard on earth. For he was taken sick and died shortly after his illness. I was informed of this by the pastor who invited me to preach; and he made the remark that it was the last sermon this man heard before going to the judgment. My subject on that occasion was the "boundless love of God".

And how true it is, my readers, that we must all appear before the judgment seat of Christ, and render our account. Certainly, if we are to meet the approbation of God, we must go along the way of the golden rule, recognizing all men as brothers, and doing unto them as we would have them do unto us. Think you that this man who did not want to hear me preach, but who heard his last sermon on earth from me, will refuse to meet me at the judgment on account of my color—something I had nothing to do with?

I am thankful to say that this unpleasant state of things which existed forty-five years ago is now numbered with the past. Since then, I have preached in many white congregations, where, I believe, all heard me gladly. In connection with my early ministry I would also mention Plymouth, Massachusetts, with its historic memories. It was here, where the Pilgrim Fathers landed and established those principles which, like the solid rock on which they stood, have defied the test of the centuries, and extended throughout the length and breadth of this great nation. May these principles ever live, and like those emanating from the impregnable Rock of Ages, produce results that shall be for the blessing of humanity. Plymouth, like many other places I have visited and labored in, is not without its incidents.

From Slave Cabin to the Pulpit

While here I was invited to make one of a party of four to attend a Sunday service at Monument Pond. When we arrived the congregation had assembled, but they had no preacher. The white brethren in my party said, "Here is a colored preacher, why not hear him."

Accordingly, I was prevailed upon to preach. The people there had never heard a colored preacher, and their curiosity was at a high pitch. Though I was somewhat of a novelty to them, they received my message, and the meeting was declared a success. At Eel River, I had what I may call a slipup—whether the name of the river had anything to do with my misfortune I am not prepared to say. I was unexpectedly called upon to preach for a white congregation, and when I got into the pulpit I could not find my text. My situation can better be imagined than described. On going home after the service I tried to describe my feelings and the circumstance of losing my text. The remark of my friend was, "Why, we would not have known it, if you had not spoken of it." While carrying on a series of meetings in the little Chapel at Plymouth, I preached on the subject of eternal punishment. There were a few in my audience who took issue with me on the subject, and we had a discussion which lasted nearly three days, they holding to the soul-sleeping doctrine, and I to the conscious existence of the soul. One of my hearers was so well pleased with my argument, that he made me a present of a valuable commentary on the New Testament.

After the discussion, I met my main antagonist—who was a clergyman— and put to him another question on the subject. He said, "I will answer you as the slave answered his master. The master had been converted, and while reading in the Epistles of Paul he came across something he did not understand, and asked his slave about it. The slave wanted to know how long he had been reading the Bible, and he said, about three weeks. 'And you have got so far as that already? Go back to the beginning and read up to that point, and you will understand it better.'" In this allusion my opponent acknowledged his deficiency on the subject.

In 1856, I was called to take charge of a small struggling church in New Haven, Connecticut, at a salary of two hundred dollars a year. At this time I was doing very well in Boston, in the way of taking care of myself and family. But feeling that this was the ordering of God, I accepted, hoping that I might be a humble instrument in His hands of doing some good among my people. I found the society in a deplorable condition and much discouraged. They reminded me of the vision of Ezekiel in the valley of dry-bones. Their views of Baptist doctrine and church government was much confused.

After much work and preaching, the dry-bones seem to get back into place and shape. The brethren not at heart Baptist, thought there was no need of a Baptist church in that vicinity, but we thought otherwise and pushed along that line. Though I had taken charge of the church, I was not ordained and could not perform the full duties of a pastor. The church urged my ordination, and I was ordained at Williamsburgh, now Brooklyn, New York.

A regular council was called according to the Baptist rule, and the ordination took place in the church of which Rev. L. A. Black was pastor. Rev. Mr. Burg, an Englishman, was the chairman of the council. Among the other members were Rev. Sampson White, and Rev. Mr. Herring. After my ordination at Williamsburgh I returned to New Haven, with all the qualifications of a regular Baptist pastor. I realized what was before me, and raised up the regular Baptist banner. I preached sermons on the subject of Baptism, prepared a special sermon on my reasons for being a Baptist and invited my outside brethren to hear it. I tried to emphasize the great commission and our Saviour's command, and that as his followers we had no right to change that command. A Methodist brother who was present, in speaking, said that he agreed with me that we had no right to change the command of Christ. Much interest was aroused by this opposition, and some of the Methodist pastors had to baptize by immersion some of their members to keep them.

I will here speak of a noticeable incident in this line. At one of my meetings a candidate presented himself for membership and wanted to be immersed. After hearing his experience, the question was asked, would he comply with the Baptist conditions of membership? He intimated that he was not ready to do so. Thereupon I refused to baptize him. He went to a Methodist minister and he agreed to perform the rite. The Methodist brother, who was better known as "Father Spence," arranged to immerse this candidate on the same Sunday that I was to baptize. There was a large crowd present in all kinds of vehicles and boats. I had led the way and buried beneath the liquid grave, those who had given evidence of their faith in Christ, and thus professed him before the world. Then came in "Father Spence," with his one candidate. This was a new departure for him and his timidity was evident. He raised his hand and said, "I baptize thee," etc., and plunged the man under the wave. For some reason or other, he lost his hold and his candidate was struggling for dear life, and came near getting drowned. The people regarded this unsuccessful attempt as a special judgment against the Methodist preacher. After this I had but little trouble about my Baptist views.

After serving the church in New Haven for one year I was compelled to resign my charge on account of pecuniary circumstances, as the church was not able to support a pastor. The sentiment of the church was much against my leaving, but I could not remain, and returned again to Boston. I am pleased to say that my stay in New Haven was not without evidence of good both to the people and to myself. I had a splendid opportunity to attend the lectures given at Yale College, and availed myself of them. So I departed from New Haven richer in knowledge and experience, if in nothing else.

I was not in Boston very long before I received another call, from a church in Newburgh, New York. This was a beautiful little town on the Hudson River, near West Point, distinguished for its relics, and as being one of the main points of operation used by General George Washington, in the Revolutionary War. It was in the year of 1858, that I received this call and settled as pastor over the church at Newburgh.

The condition of the flock was similar to that in which I found the church in New Haven. With this addition, however, they seem to be of Dutch origin and peculiarities, and were destitute of what most colored people needed at that time, and even now, an education. The non-progress of my people in this country is due to the fact that they are not educated.

The confused state and condition of the colored people in Newburgh prevented the growth and development of the spiritual fruit that one had a right to look for. It was my duty to faithfully sow the seed that another might reap the desired harvest. This I endeavored to do, to the best of my ability, and leaving the result with Him who knows all things.

I have no remarkable incidents to relate during my stay in this place save one or two. I was invited on one occasion to preach for a brother minister. When I arrived at his meeting-house I found it crowded with both white and colored people. The former being mostly young men.

The crowd had come together doubtless, expecting to have what they call a good time. After a little while the pastor whispered to me, saying, "There has been an announcement made that a sermon would be preached here, on the great day of judgment." He wanted to know from me if I could preach on that subject. I told him it was quite a short notice, but I thought I could do so; anyway, I would try.

He went on with the preliminary part of the service, and at the time for the sermon, I arose and stepped forward with my text: "The great day of his wrath has come, and who shall be able to stand?" As I was getting along, in the midst of my sermon, I noticed quite a number of the white young men, who came looking for fun, leaving. As they did not see anybody jump up, or falling over the benches, they were doubtless disappointed and took their departure.

I afterward learned from some of his members that the pastor did not have the best motive in view, in forcing me to take this subject without a moment's notice. Many, however, pronounced the sermon good, and some dated their conversion to the same. In this incident, I was reminded of that Scripture where it says that God causes the wrath of men to praise him.

From Slave Cabin to the Pulpit

I shall never forget my visit to Snake Hill, which is just three miles from Newburgh. The origin of the name seems to be founded on fact, as tradition gives it. It is reported that on a certain day a big show was in town, and most of its curiosities consisted of snakes. The authorities of the town ordered that these reptiles should be loosed, and they found their home in the hill that afterward assumed the name. On the day that I visited this mountain in company with others, these reptiles probably had concealed themselves in the caves, for not many were visible.

The most interesting thing to me on this mountain was the heavy black cloud which seemed about to burst on us at any moment. We did not get any of the shower while on the mountain, but when we came down we found it had rained considerable. This taught one the lesson that it is one thing to be on the mountain, another thing to be in the valley.

On one occasion, I happened in the court house here, and was conversing with a white man on the subject of religion, when another informed me if I had anything to do with politics, I would soon find myself in the jail. He may have said this in the way of a joke, but in those times, many a true thing was said in a joke. In closing I can say this about Newburgh, that I have nothing to regret relative to my stay there. I had many warm friends, and pleasant remembrances of the place.

CHAPTER VI.

IN A VIRGINIA PULPIT.

I NOW propose to speak concerning my preparation and work at Richmond, Virginia. And here I may say, that like General Grant, Benj. F. Butler, and other Northern generals, I made several attempts and was much delayed before I got there.

When I left my charge in Newburgh, N. Y., I returned to Boston and remained about two years. During this time I was engaged in a small newspaper business and preached for the Old Ladies' Home, then located on Phillip Street. For my two years' service to them I received no compensation. But I shall never forget what the matron, Mrs. Martha Thurston, a devout Christian woman, said to me in regard to my pay. In speaking of my service she remarked: "Brother Randolph, we shall never be able to pay you for your services here, but the Lord will reward you."

I believe her prayer was answered. A few days after this I went into the well-known store of Hitchcook & Potter, and was introduced to Mr. J. C. Lester of Boston, as the preacher at the Colored Old Ladies' Home. He asked several questions, and among others, how much money I received for my services. Of course, I told him. He was surprised, and asked how I managed to live, and finished by saying, "If the men in this store will give you a barrel of flour, I will take it home for you." This was said in the way of a joke. But a few days after I was invited to call at the store again, and received in money the value of a barrel of flour. I speak of this to show the answer to faithful prayer, and also for the purpose of introducing my friend, Mr. J. C. Lester, who assisted me to Richmond.

I must now hasten on to Richmond, the scene of conflict, for I will be delayed somewhat on my journey. As I was in Boston during the latter part of the War, it was my cherished desire to go and serve my country as chaplain in one of the colored regiments. Accordingly I offered myself to Governor Andrew, but there was no opening at the time for me. When Lee surrendered to Grant at Appomattox, and the war was declared at an end, and the slaves free, many of the freedmen in Virginia—those who knew they were free—gathered at the great centres where the Union Soldiers were quartered, mainly for protection from their masters, and to see what freedom meant.

One of these places was City Point, Virginia. As there was a large number of men, women and children quartered here, and were in the condition of sheep, without pasture or shepherd, I was urged by Rev. L. A. Grimes, to look after and try and help these poor people. But I had not the necessary means to undertake this work. I presented the matter to my friend, Mr. Lester, and he with others furnished the desired help.

On my journey I stopped at Baltimore, Md., and during my delay, the nation was thrown in the deepest sorrow over the reported news that President Lincoln had been assassinated. The national flag was lowered at half-mast, proving that the report was true. I remained in Baltimore until after the funeral and then hastened to City Point. On arriving I found the colored people as I have intimated, in a confused state, and wanted more than I was able to give them. My stay at City Point was short, for I realized that that was not the best place for me to make my headquarters. As the way to Richmond had opened and hostilities ceased, I hastened to establish myself there as a place more suited for the work, in every way.

On my arrival at Richmond I was met at the Rocketts, by Filds Cook, and carried to the house of Mr. John Adams, who had cognizance of my coming. He was one of the most prominent colored men in the city, having been a freeman before the war, and was in fair circumstances. Being in his hands I was taken good care of, and was able to proceed at once to the needed work. The scene that opened before my eyes as I entered Richmond cannot be accurately described by word or pen. The city was in smoke and ashes, that is, a goodly part of it, for the Confederacy, on taking their departure, fired the city rather than let it fall into the hands of the Union forces.

The colored people from all parts of the state were crowding in at the capital, running, leaping, and praising God that freedom had come at last. It seems to me I can hear their songs now as they ring through the air: "Slavery chain done broke at last; slavery chain done broke at last—I's goin' to praise God till I die."

Many of the old people had prayed and looked forward to this day, but like Moses they were permitted to see it afar off, and not enter it.

The place was literally full of soldiers, "Yanks" and "Rebs."

The armies were breaking up and returning home. Richmond was the great centre for dispersions, all hours, day and night was the marching of regiments, going and coming. The sight of some of these would bring tears to the dryest eyes, as they beheld men wounded, maimed in every possible shape and form that could be mentioned. And many of these, like the poor colored people, were truly glad that the war was over.

The city of Richmond did not have accommodations enough for this great mass of colored people, so many were gathered on the suburbs and taken care of in the best why possible under the circumstances.

One of these principal camps, where the people were huddled in temporary structures, was called Schinnborazzo. Here I spent a part of my first Sunday in Richmond, and preached to a large congregation. Religious services were held in these camps all day, and several other preachers were present and readily lent their service. Among these was Rev. John Jasper, who has distinguished himself since, as the famous "Sun do move preacher." This was the first time I had the pleasure of meeting him. His preaching was much more excitable than mine, and seemed to effect the people in a way that I could not. This scene, and the day's work, was very impressive upon me, and made me feel and sympathize with these folks only as one who had been in slavery, could feel and sympathize.

It had been argued by some that, if the Negroes were set free they would murder and kill the white people. But instead of that, they were praising God and the Yankees for life and liberty. Of course, soldiers were stationed about these camps, and in all the streets of the city, to keep in check anything like an outbreak. I am sorry to say here, that the treatment of some of the soldiers toward the poor colored people was indeed shameful. For the slightest provocation, and sometimes for no cause whatever, the butts of their guns and bayonets were used unmercifully upon them.

The colored people held indignation meetings, resolutions were passed, and a. delegation appointed to lay this whole matter before President Johnson. I was the instigator of the meeting being called. And not until these steps were taken did the colored people have rest from the ill-treatment of the soldiers.

This, also, must be said, relative to these soldiers: the most of them who committed these depredations were from the Middle States, and sympathizers with the South. They seemed to be mad because the "negger" was free, and took the authority given them by the wearing of the blue to express it.

The petition of the colored men was noticed by the President, and remedied by General Schofield. In addition to the Provost Marshal's, where soldiers were disciplined, bureaus were established for the freedmen, where they could be heard and assisted. The true condition of the colored people at this time will never be written. When I arrived at Richmond, I had letters of introduction from Governor Andrew to Governor Pierpont, and also to General Schofield. I was appointed by the General to issue tickets or passes, and distribute them to the people, in order that they might get what provisions and clothing there was for them through the agency of the bureau. It was a sight to behold to see these hungry souls crowding in at my office to obtain the slips of paper that was to give them the necessities of life. The Freedman's Bureau also took the place of the Court House, to protect and settle all difficulties that might arise among the people.

In this particular some of the incidents were heartrending, the most severe cases being where the former master and slave were concerned. Some of the masters were very reluctant in giving up their servants, and tried to defraud and rob them out of their freedom, and many of the slaves had to run away from their masters to be free. It is true that the proclamation had been accepted, and Lee had surrendered his sword to Grant, but some of the white people still contended that "these are my neggers."

When some of the white people found that they could no longer retain them as slaves they used them very cruelly. I was often called at the bureau to interest myself in and defend these poor people. One sad case I will here mention—a colored girl about eighteen years of age, who was brought before the bureau, with a charge against her former master. She had been shamefully whipped and her back burned with a hot iron. I well recall the words of General Merrett, who was at the time the president of the bureau.

As he beheld the condition of this girl, he exclaimed, "What is this!" The officer who had her in charge said, "It is the devil." An eye-witness who was present photographed the back of this girl, and it can be had if my readers would like to see it. Let me make another brief mention, in the South, especially during the dark days of slavery. The colored man was expected to stop and let the white person pass first, and often had to get off the sidewalk to let the white woman pass. I was an eye-witness to this incident: A white woman was about to cross the street, but the colored teamster, who had the right of way, did not stop for her to cross. She had him arrested for attempting to run over her. I went to the jail, and on my personal testimony, he was released.

This simply illustrates the condition of things that I speak of, and also the necessity and work of the Freedman's Bureau.

The Freedman's Bureau was only a temporary arrangement intended to help relieve the condition of the ex-slaves. While it had the means to do so it was inestimable to the poor and needy. But soon the sources of supply failed and the important work was abandoned.

From Slave Cabin to the Pulpit

This made the suffering and needs of the people more intense than ever. Many had to go back to their former masters to work or starve, and many of the whites tried to make the Negroes feel that freedom was worse than slavery.

In slavery times the masters would see to it, that the slaves were fed—that is, with such as they had to give them, but now, they would see them starve. It is not hard to understand this state of affairs, when one thinks of the situation; here the whites were smarting under their defeat, the Negroes, who were their main support, were taken away from them as slaves and goods of chattel, but still remained at their doors. The unvented wrath they had for the Yankees, for meddling with their pet institution, was poured out on the poor Negroes.

When the bureau closed, the Police Court took its place as a tribunal of justice. I have already stated, that the Freedman's Bureau was not only a place for relief, but also, for the distribution of justice. I will speak briefly of the Police Court, that took its place, and my relation with the same.

In the return and establishment of the Police Court, the Mayor of the city for the time being was constituted the judge. This happened to be George C. Cabooses, a New Yorker. He studied law in the office of Chief Justice Chase, and was a man of excellent qualities.

The white South looked upon him, however, as a northern carpetbagger, and did everything to oppose him. He was a faithful administer of the law as he understood it, was patient and full of justice. The colored people, as well as the white, who had violated the law, in his opinion, had to pay the penalty. The court was constantly crowded with colored people with their complaints. I was invited by Mr. Cahoone to look after the interests of these people, for they needed some one who could understand them. I accepted the invitation and was frequently in the court. Many would come to Mr. Cahoone, with their long story, but he would say to them, "You go and tell Mr. Randolph, and he will tell me." After I had heard the long complaint, I would put it in as short a form as possible and then explain it to the judge. There was no end to complaints and outrages committed on the poor and ignorant. If the farmer lost his horse, cow, dog or chicken, by death, or theft, the "negger" was held responsible, and arrested on the least suspicion.

I remember a special case, where a man lost his cow by death, and two colored men were accused of it. The evidence showed that they were innocent of the cow's death; but the case had to go to the higher court. I appeared there in their behalf, and they were acquitted.

The object of many of these arrests can be fully understood by the Southern people only.

The Negro had suddenly been made a citizen and given the right of franchise; this was an offence to the Southern white people—and one that they will never forgive the North for. In my opinion it should be overlooked just as other war measures are overlooked and forgiven, for it was a necessity.

The white people were determined to prevent them from voting, if they could, and various methods were resorted to, in order to deprive them of their vote. Chief among these, was to get the men put in jail on some criminal charge, and thus disqualify them; for the law considered all disqualified who had been arrested. The jail house and chain-gang were constantly filled with able-bodied colored men whose offence did not entitle them to be there. The ballot, though a great privilege, was the cause of much suffering for the freedmen.

Before I dismiss these court proceedings let me mention one more case in which I had to participate. On one occasion, Mr. Cahoone was absent and his assistant was on the bench. This morning without much delay or inquiry, the judge pro tem— had sentenced a colored boy to prison for stealing a small sum of money. As I entered I saw the boy standing and weeping bitterly. I interrogated him and found that the man who had brought the charge against him was his father. I sought out the father and found him to be a white man. Several who were in the position to know, verified the statement of the lad that the man was his father. I made known the facts in the case and urged the judge to delay the case until he heard me.

I endeavored to show in my argument, that this was a case where a father was appearing against his own son, and though his mother was colored and had been sold in slavery, nevertheless this was his flesh and blood. The judge stopped me before I finished my argument, by saying "That will do Sir; I will revoke the sentence, and you can take the boy in charge for three weeks." This is one of many cases of this kind that might be mentioned, but the white South rarely likes to discuss this part of the question. Mr. Cahoone, in spite of his acts of kindness and justice to all, was unable to win over as his friends the local white people.

They looked upon him as a Northern Carpet-bagger, and were determined to get rid of him, if possible. They watched for their chance as a cat would watch for a rat. An unfortunate circumstance with which Mr. Cahoone was connected, furnished an opportunity for them to commence operations.

A foreigner died without a proper will; and in such cases the effects go to the state. But Mr. Cahoone acting not as the mayor of the city, but as a lawyer, examined the submitted report and ordered it to be collected, signing his name in approval of the same as a proper document, and received the lawyer's fee for his work.

When the time came for his re-election, this matter was strongly urged against him on the ground of forgery. He was elected, however, by an overwhelming majority of the votes of colored and union men. This incensed the whites; they destroyed the ballot-boxes and votes, and proceeded to eject the incumbent and appoint another in his place. Mr. Cahoone remonstrated against such procedure, for he was a man of strong convictions and was not afraid to express them.

The crisis was now at hand. The local whites who held office under him deserted at this trying hour, and he was compelled to depend solely on the colored men and a few unionists. The mob surrounded him and his colored followers in a hall and kept them there all day.

It was necessary for him to appeal to the United States authorities for protection, and also to decide who was the rightful incumbent of the office. The decision was in favor of Mr. Cahoone, and he was restored to his former position. In this trial judge Underwood presided, and he was defended by Henry A. Wise, Ex-Governor Wells, and Chandler of Maine.

The whites were determined, however, not to let Mr. Cahoone remain in office. The charge of forgery relative to the report he had signed, was repeated against him. He was arrested, and tried by the Court of Virginia, found guilty, and sentenced, but Governor Walker, of Virginia, would not see this noble man go to the penitentiary, and therefore pardoned him. After this he took his departure from Virginia, the scene of trial and persecution. It should be understood here, that the colored people did not desert Mr. Cahoone, but supported him to the last, and many suffered with him. I was personally acquainted with one man who was shot. I myself visited him while he was in jail, and heard him, with tears in his eyes, speak of the sad disappointment of justice and cruel treatment he had received at the hands of the southern white people.

In beginning this chapter, and speaking of my advent in Richmond, I referred to the condition of the people generally as I found them. How the soldiers were passing and repassing for days and weeks. In this connection I wanted to say, that one of the chief divisions was General Sherman's. It was a wonderful sight to see this army passing for three long days, and colored people standing in the streets with buckets of water to refresh them as they passed. White and colored people alike were surprised to see so many "Yankees," and they commonly remarked, "Where did they come from? They must come from under the ground."

Also, I want to emphasize another point in connection with this early state of affairs; and that is, the ideas that many of the freedmen had relative to the new state of things. The current view among many, directly after the war was, that they would receive so much land from the government to help them in the new life. This opinion seemed reasonable, and was shared by many. But imagine their disappointment when they were told frankly that the government had no such intentions as they entertained. Well do I remember the impression made on the people when Senator Henry Wilson, on his visit to Richmond, and at the invitation of the colored delegation, answered this question. The kind Senator did not leave them without some good advice. They were not looking for advice, however, but land to plant corn and potatoes, for their wives and children. The condition, as I have intimated, of these people was deplorable. Instead of forty acres and a mule, they had to return to their former masters barefooted, and hat in hand, and ask permission to work for "victuals and clothes". When this part of the freedman's condition is considered rightfully there will be an opportunity for regrets and tears of repentance. Is there a case in all history, that can be compared with this, where over four millions of people, ignorant and empty-handed, are turned loose into the world to seek for themselves homes in the face of every possible disadvantage?

During the time Pierpont was governor of Virginia, a report came from Chester County, that the Negroes in that vicinity were in a state of insurrection, and that they were about to rise up and kill all the white people in that section. I was acquainted with the governor through my letter of introduction from Governor Andrew.

As there was considerable talk about this uprising, Mr. Pierpont requested my views on the subject. I informed him that I was in a position to know, if there was anything of the kind, but did not believe that there was a word of truth in the report; but that it was rather a pretext gotten up on the part of the whites to murder the colored people. The governor paid no attention to the rumor, by sending militia, and there was no riot. A few colored men were out hunting rebels, and the whites cried, "Negro uprising."

This is a good illustration of many reported uprisings among the colored people of the South. Usually these reports originated among the white and not the colored people. This is one of the sham tricks of the South, to get up a Negro riot, call out the militia or the citizens in arms to butcher the blacks, for the purpose of keeping them in their places, as they say.

Of course there are good white people in the South, who took no part in these cruel outrages against the colored people. But they are to be criticised because they do not condemn them.

Every community is held responsible that permits one class of its citizens to outrage another class with impunity.

Hundreds of colored people in the South, since emancipation, have been whipped to death, lynched, and burned alive, until the question is asked, and asked rightfully, "Is the South civilized?"

What Thomas Jefferson said about slavery, so I repeat in substance, relative to the persecution of my people: "I tremble for my country when I think that God is just."

While speaking on this subject of southern outrages, permit me to say this also: that I believe much responsibility rests on the North in regard to this whole matter. The North should not be content as long as one man is oppressed, and his rights disregarded. If she is inclined to be negligent in this matter, let her remember the two hundred thousand colored soldiers who died in the defence of the Union, and the multitudes of white soldiers who were saved from death-traps, and starvation, by the hands of the poor slave.

The covenant that General B. F. Butler made with himself when he walked among so many dead and brave black soldiers, should be the sentiment of the whole North; never to forget them, or be untrue.

During my stay in Richmond as pastor and carrying on special work among the freedmen, it was my privilege to meet several of the most prominent men. Among these was Judge John C. Underwood, of the United States District Court.

He was a good, kind-hearted man, and took much interest in the colored people. Often I had to consult with him about local matters. On one occasion he sent for me, and I was to meet him at his boarding-place, which was the Spots Woods Hotel, the most popular hotel in the city. I called at the hotel, entered the bar-room, and enquired for him of the bar-keeper, but he made no reply to my direct question. Finally he said, "If you take off your hat I'll answer you." I had just returned from Boston, and had on a new beaver hat. "Why, sir," said I, a little indignant at his gruff remark, "take off my hat in a barroom! The other gentlemen have on their hats, and they do not look half as good as mine." His blunt reply was, "But neggers take off theirs." "I am a gentleman, sir," said I.

The gentleman behind the bar ordered me out, and if I had not obeyed he would have had me and my new silk hat out on the sidewalk, upside down, and I couldn't have helped myself. The good judge was provoked when he heard of the occurrence. But this was Richmond, and not Boston. Before I left Richmond I saw this hotel in ashes, and its bare walls standing white against the sun. When I saw this, it was natural for me to think of the insult I received there, but with no malice in my heart, for I pitied and felt sorry for the poor drunken set, caught there on that fatal night, and whose bodies furnished fuel for the flames. Fifteen or more bodies were found in the ruins beyond identification.

Here we were brought face to face with the great evil of intemperance. And also the fact that the popular hotel is often the source and the end of the evil. The sight of that fire haunts me now as I think of those human beings, standing at the windows crying for help and no one able to help them.

The Rev. Dr. Dickenson, D.D., editor of the Religious Herald, was also another man of note, that I met while in Richmond. Soon after my arrival, I called on him in company with a friend, who introduced me as a preacher from Boston. At that time the mention of the name Boston was sufficient to stir the iron in any southern white man's blood. For she had taken the lead in the antislavery struggles and was the first to raise her hand against the Rebellion.

So, naturally, he expressed himself quite forcibly in regard to the Massachusetts people, and his general views on the subject of slavery from the southern stand-point. I endeavored to keep my voice under, being reminded of that scripture which said: "A soft answer turneth away wrath, but grievous words stir up anger." The doctor felt that the North had committed the unpardonable sin, and there was no forgiveness for them. When I met him again, it was in Boston, at a minister's conference. In addressing the conference, he said in substance that it was a great blessing to the South that slavery was abolished, and it was worth all it had to pay for it, of blood and treasure. He also intimated that he would help to lift up the Negro. I had the pleasure of speaking after him, and referred to our first meeting in Richmond, but did not allude to his views at that time. I was glad to see that he was a converted man, and was able to look at things in a new light.

Dr. Jeter was another popular and very distinguished personage in and about Richmond. He was a good preacher and theologian. I became acquainted with him in my early ministry at the Ebenezer church. He used to drop in occasionally to hear me preach, and would sit right in front of me where he could see and nod his head to all with which he assented. After hearing me on one occasion he made the remark, that I was as good a colored preacher as he ever heard, and he was proud of me, because I was born in Virginia. I suppose every man should be proud of his birth-place. I am grateful for all the good that Virginia has done me; but I cannot boast very much in this direction, when I remember that her laws forbade me to read the Bible. I feel more indebted to Massachusetts for what I am than I do to Virginia.

I had to flee from my natural mother, Virginia, and seek protection under my adopted mother, Massachusetts. I think I love my adopted mother the best.

In conversation with Dr. Jeter on the subject of slavery, he once remarked, that he believed slavery to be right and a divine institution, because the Bible supported it. He was not particular in quoting that passage, that God had made of one blood all the nations of the earth, or where Christ teaches, "that we must do unto our neighbors as we would have them do unto us."

While he maintained these views and endeavored to support them by scripture, yet he said, "I hope I am wrong in my views." I did not understand why he should make such a remark, unless it was that he felt the compunctions of conscience.

I was informed that when the Union soldiers were approaching Richmond, the good doctor intimated his willingness to go out and fight the Yankees. He put on his confederate armor and went forth, but he did not get near enough for anyone to hurt him, or he to hurt anyone else. The doctor was tall and thin, and had very good legs for running. So while he was a good preacher and theologian, and believed in slavery as a divine institution, yet he was a poor soldier. His position reminds me of the quaker in the duel. As the opponents had to choose weapons, the Quaker selected as his, a long-range rifle, and his antagonist pistols. In approaching each other the Quaker said, "Stand thou there, for thou art near enough for me to hit thee." The other man withdrew, fearing that while the Quaker was near enough with his rifle, he was not near enough with his pistol. So the doctor doubtless found the Yankees' guns too long and effectual for him to face.

Rev. R. Riland, D.D., was another important character whom I wish to mention in this connection. He was the pastor of what was known as the Old African Baptist Church, of Richmond. The membership of this church was all colored people, and was reported to be between three and four thousand. Mr Riland was the white pastor over this colored flock. In the days of slavery the colored pastor was unknown, the spiritual adviser and teacher was always a white man. There were colored exhorters and class leaders, but the boss preacher was always white. My first meeting of Dr. Riland was in the First African Church. I was introduced as the pastor of the Ebenezer Baptist Church; after the introduction I noticed he wanted to say something, so I commenced the conversation by asking him how many persons he thought the edifice would hold. "About fifteen hundred," was his answer. I expressed surprise, and asked him how it was that the reported membership was so large and the seating capacity so small. He thought I was a northern man, bred and born, and went on to explain that a large number of his congregation had gone South—meaning of course, that they were sold in slavery.

He proceeded, also, to tell how mild the form of slavery was in Virginia, compared with other parts of the South, supposing I knew nothing of it. I made a long sigh, and remarked that if Hell was any worse than slavery in Virginia, I did not want to go there. "Why," said he, "what do you mean?" I repeated again, and said that what I meant was, that slavery was a torment in Virginia. I then proceeded to tell him that I was a Virginian by birth, and had lived for years within her borders and tasted much of the bitter cup of slavery, and also showed him just what the true relation between the master and the slave was. When I got through he had but very little to say on the subject.

When David saw a bear or lion in his flock, he rose up and slew it. The lions and bears of slavery entered Dr. Riland's flock more than once, and took away his lambs; but he never was known to complain, or to make a single protest. How he will explain and settle this matter with the great Shepherd and Bishop of souls, I cannot now say. Yet it is not my purpose to sit in judgment upon him, for he had many good characteristics, and I had a good chance to learn of them, for I was a pupil under him in Dr. Colver's school.

This school was established at the close of the war for the benefit of the colored ministers, and Nathaniel Colver, D.D., former pastor of Tremont Temple, Boston, was the President.

Mr. Riland was employed in this school because of his long intimate relation with the colored people as pastor. He was kind and patient, and a good biblical scholar, and as students we all loved him, regardless of his slave-holding proclivities.

One remarkable thing about this school was, it was held in what was known as "Lumpkins Jail". This at one time was the greatest slave market in the world. Virginia furnished most of the slaves for the other Southern States, and this was the great place where they were sold on the auction block to the highest bidder. The groans and expressions of sorrow, that used to go up from this accursed spot, when husbands and wives, parents and children, were separated never more to meet, cannot be described by tongue or pen.

How fitting it was that a school for the instruction of the freedmen, and especially the Christian ministry, should be erected, and occupy this place; verifying that scripture, that God makes even the wrath of men to praise him.

Let me recall, also, two other characters I met in Richmond during my stay there; though they are not as distinguished as those I have mentioned, yet they have left upon me as strong an impression as any.

The first of these two that I desire to speak of, is Uncle Phil. Jones. It was over sixteen years since I had seen him, on the old plantation in the days of cruel slavery. I had left the South for the North, in order to obtain my freedom; now, I had returned as a teacher and preacher of glad tidings. Uncle Phil. Jones had known me from childhood, and naturally enough when he heard of me in Richmond his great joy was to see me and take me by the hand. I shall never forget that meeting, as the old man approached me with head white as cotton, tottering feet and trembling hand.

"Why, Peter! is this you? Praise the Lord that I have lived to see the day."

Then he burst into tears and sobs. It was an effecting scene. Poor old man, time and slavery had dealt hard with him, and left the visible marks. I, myself, had seen this old man's back literally furrowed by the overseer's lash, and washed in salt water to preserve it, and keep away the flies.

And now, like a horse that has been worked nearly to death for all that he is worth, until he becomes old, crippled and poor, this poor old man is turned loose without corn or fodder, on the cold charities of the world. Who are to blame for his destitute condition, himself, his parents, or those who have driven him until they could drive him no longer?

In connection with Uncle Phil. Jones, I may also relate that I met in Richmond, his master, William B. Harrison. This is the same man who was mentioned in my little book on slave life, as helping the sixty-six in obtaining our freedom. Though ho was by no means an angel toward his own slaves, yet he was friendly and kind toward us in securing our rights. I called on Mr. Harrison in Richmond. He seemed glad to see me, and had much to say about the unjust treatment we received at the hands of the lawyer and the executors. But he, too, like Phil. Jones, had experienced a great change. He was not the William B. Harrison that once I knew on the James River, with his well-stocked plantation and over a hundred slaves. These all, like a dream of the night, had suddenly vanished from his gaze. He was a great enemy of the North and fought for all he was worth, and in return the Yankees spared neither him nor his chickens.

I met, also, William Allen, better known as Major Allen. He was a wealthy nephew of my master, who raised and equipped a southern regiment for the rebellion. He invited me to see him, and was pleased to tell his friends that I had been a servant in his family. I do not know why he took so much pleasure in mentioning it. I cannot say that I was ashamed of what happened to be my misfortune. Joseph was a servant in Egypt, but in due time his position was changed and he was a blessing to all succeeding generations. The Major had obtained his wealth from Colonel William Allen, the owner of the celebrated "Clearmount Plantation," on the James River, who was estimated to own nearly a thousand slaves.

"Old Joe Mayo," as he was commonly called by the colored people of Richmond, also deserves mention in these brief records. The colored people looked upon him as their Nero, a man without a heart. He was a tobacco manufacturer, making the famous Virginia Navy Brand. He was the mayor of the city when Richmond surrendered to the Union forces.

From Slave Cabin to the Pulpit

He had made his boast, however, that before he would surrender he would ride in blood up to his saddle. This statement is something like that made by the boy who said he was going to curse his master; he went to the big gate and cursed his master, but at the time his master was miles away. The Yankees were miles away when Mr. Mayo made this remark, but when they got to the gates of Richmond, he was among the first to flee for safety. Doubtless, he changed his mind and thought that discretion was the better part of valor.

I was told by one who knew from bitter experience, that when Mr. Mayo became mayor of the city he gave it out, that he had a whipping for "every negger in town". It was his law that every colored person who was caught on the streets without a pass, was to be sent to the jail and receive nine and thirty lashes.

This public whipping in the jail was not altogether like a circus or a picnic—the more times you went to it the more you wanted to go. But the opposite was true: the strongest and stoutest, after they had embraced the whipping-post, and received what was for them, rarely cared to visit that place again. A colored woman with her child in her arms was on the streets without a pass; it is said that Mr. Mayo slapped the child's face and sent the woman to the whipping-post, thereby, verifying his statement, that he had a whipping for every "negger in town".

There was a time when Nero no longer sat on the throne with undisputed sway; his sceptre of power had departed. So with Mr. Mayo when I first saw him in Richmond. His fine residence, where the silver had been buried in the garden—but not so deep that the Yankees could not find it—was occupied by General Roberts, and Mr. E. D. Bean, of the New Hampshire second Regiment. As I beheld him, he excited my sympathy and pity; and I was reminded of the words of the sacred poet: "O Lucifer, thou Son of the morning, how hast thou fallen." Yes, and fallen never to rise again. The old man died and was buried. But the colored people looked on his grave without a tear, and though there was no epitaph written on his tombstone, they could easily supply it by saying:

"Here lies I 'old Joe Mayo' in his grave dead,
Often he whipped us till we bled.
He will send us no more to the whipping-post,
For he has gone to join the silent host.
To the judgment seat he must come
To give account for the deeds he has done."

Doubtless my readers will be pleased to hear something about the first political meeting I attended after the war, in Richmond. There was much excitement about this time, for the smell of powder was still in the air. A meeting was called by the Union people—including, of course, the colored—to consider plans for a new constitution. The big meeting was in the capitol, the late seat of the head of the Confederacy. This was sacred ground made hallowed because of the distinguished Virginians and statesmen who had stood there. It was a thing unknown for a colored man to stand in those halls and on those steps to mingle his voice with the great men of the past.

He was known to tread upon those sacred precincts, only as a slave and servant, and never as a man advocating the rights of man. I took my place at the head of the big steps with the white Union men. My colored friends thought I was running a great risk by making myself so conspicuous when it was known that I came from Boston. I must confess that I did feel a little weak in the knees, for I did not know at what time a stray bullet might come my way, and rebuke me for daring to occupy a position that no other colored man had assumed. Finally I was called upon to address the assembly. I need not say there was silence, for all eyes were turned toward me, and they were anxious to hear what the colored man had to say.

I began my remarks, by saying that I was a Virginian by birth, and only a son of Massachusetts by adoption; that I had to leave Virginia to obtain and enjoy my freedom, and I had returned for the purpose of helping to build up my native state, so that she might form an important link in the great bond of Union. When the whites heard I was born in Virginia they seemed more anxious to hear me. I continued further by saying, that what we the colored people wanted, was money and education, so that we could own railroads and steamboats. And that when we came in possession of these we would have the white people to ride beside us and not behind us. When the meeting was over several of the local whites congratulated me, and offered to treat me with cigars, and so forth, but I politely declined.

It has been over a quarter of a century since I in a jocose manner made this brief allusion to the needs of the colored people. And this same idea might be emphasized to-day with greater earnestness and sincerity. My brethren in the South to-day, are dying by the wholesale for the want of the necessities and comforts of life, and this is due to the fact that they have not been educated to provide for themselves.

Give them education and money, and many of the unpleasant phases that now exist relative to the Negro would be unknown. Those few who, by hard struggle and opposition, have acquired education and money, are better respected by the whites. This is true in the church, and all the avenues of life.

A brief incident to illustrate this fact may be in order here.

A story is related of a prominent New York layman, who invited a colored merchant to his church and a seat in his pew. When this black cloud entered the church the true spirit of worship, for the time being, seemed to have taken its flight. The congregation could not worship in the spirit on account of the presence of this dark intruder. The minister was hindered in his discourse because he saw that his congregation was offended.

At the close of the service the offending member was reproved by another for bringing this dark stranger into his pew. The layman defended himself by replying that the stranger was a Christian and an educated man. "No matter," was the reply, "he is a Negro, and let him go to his own church."

"But he is a rich Negro, and has arrived with a valuable cargo," continued the merchant. "Indeed," said the fault-finding brother;

"give me an introduction." The moment he said rich Negro that was a horse of another color, and sufficient to cause a change of opinion. So I repeat, give the colored man money and education and he will be recognized the world over.

In speaking of the causes which lead to the ignorant and degrading condition of the colored people in this country, I think I can safely say that they themselves are not wholly responsible. For they have lived for centuries in a country rich in resources; through their sweat and blood others have become rich and powerful, but they poor and weak. As the whole country aided in the oppression, the whole country is partly responsible for their present condition.

CHAPTER VII.

RELIGIOUS CONDITION.

IN the previous chapter I spoke more directly concerning the political and social environments of the colored people in Richmond, as I found them at the close of the war. In this chapter I wish to speak more definitely concerning their religious condition. I arrived in Richmond twenty-five days after the surrender, and was there only two weeks when I was invited to assume the pastorate of the Ebenezer Baptist Church. I accepted the same for three months' trial, and at the expiration of that time was duly called as the regular pastor. This was at the beginning of an important era in the religious history of the colored people.

This church, as well as others through the South, had never had a colored pastor. He who was considered the under-Shepherd and was expected to lead his flock into the green pastures, and beside the still waters, was always white. Why the colored people should now change their old pastors for new ones, may be more easily imagined than described. But this must be said, that the colored people as a whole, had but little confidence and faith in their white pastors as religious leaders. They rather looked upon them as parts of the machinery that belonged to slavery, and regarded them more as religious bosses, whose duty it was to keep them in their places by persuading them to be contented with their present lot and obey their masters in the flesh, for such was well pleasing to God. Now they were free and had a voice in selecting their pastor, it is not unreasonable to suppose, that they wanted a pastor who could sympathize with them in their afflictions, and remember the bondman as bound with him. They wanted one who could preach without fear, not only on obedience but on love, the Fatherhood of God, and the Brotherhood of man, and how Christ came to deliver the captive, and set the bondman free. On such topics as the foregoing the white pastor always had to touch lightly, for fear of losing his official head.

In this new state of affairs naturally new difficulties arose. There were no colored preachers educated and trained in the South for this important trust and responsibility. Whatever qualifications I had for the pastorate, and my ideas of the church polity, had all been received in the North and not from the South.

I was brought immediately face to face with strange customs and trying difficulties.

I found that the male and female members of the church were not allowed to sit together on the same side of the church. When the husband and wife entered the vestibule of the church, they separated, the husband going in at one door to his side of the house, and the wife going in at another door to her side of the house. Likewise the mother and son, the bridal couple, the lover and the loved, all had to conform to this rule. I condemned and ridiculed such a custom as a relic of slavery, and soon had the families sitting together, and the young men with the young ladies whom they accompanied to church.

This was a new state of things, and soon my church was named the "aristocratic church".

The women were allowed no part in the church meetings. I tried to show that the women bore the greater part of the burden and expenses of the church, and as members they were entitled to recognition. Before I left the church the women not only had a voice, but voted in the business meetings.

One of the most perplexing difficulties I met with at the beginning of my religious work in the South was the "Marriage Question". Not that phase of the question that is often debated—"Is marriage a failure?" but how to join together those who wanted to be joined in matrimony. During the days of slavery slaves were married according to the state law, but lived together more on the concubinage order. The husband and wife, after living together long enough to have children, were often separated and sold into different parts of the South, never to see each other again. And thus separated they were encouraged to marry again, and raise children for the slave-market. As I have intimated, Virginia, and Richmond especially, was the great slave-market that furnished the majority of the slaves for the rest of the South.

Now that freedom had been proclaimed throughout the land, hundreds of those who had been separated returned to their former home. But they found their former companions married again—they of course expecting never to see them again. Now here came the difficulty; as the marriage of the slaves consisted only in common consent among themselves and their masters, the state law had nothing to do with it. Therefore special legislative enactment had to be made to meet the case; thereupon the legislature passed a law, recognizing all living together as man and wife. After this they had to be married according to the state law. Just before and after this enactment a large number came to me to be married, seven and eight couples a night.

The perplexing part was, as I have intimated, to determine which were the right ones to marry. This state of things existed not only in Virginia, but all through the South. There was great need of competent pastors to meet this, and other phases of religious work. Accordingly, several who were thought to be fitted for the work, were set apart and ordained to the ministry with the authority to marry, the Freedman's Bureau granting them the proper license to perform the ceremony. I might here mention a few of the many who were at that time set apart for the work. Rev. Richard Wells, who succeeded me as pastor of the Ebenezer, and is still pastor at this writing; Rev. Fields Cook, Rev. Scott Goffney, Rev. John Jasper, who has attracted the attention of the world with his idea that the sun moves round the earth; Rev. W. Robinson, Rev. John White, Rev. Ned Jentry, Rev. Jordan Smith, and others.

These men have had good records, and accomplished much for their race.

I must say that my work at the Ebenezer was one of joy as well as difficulty. It was my pleasure to receive many into the church by baptism, and during my four and one half years' pastorate to see the membership increase from six hundred, to fourteen hundred.

During my stay with the church I had several of my white friends from Boston, Mass., to visit me, and see the nature of the work I was doing. It may not be out of the way here for me to mention a few names in this connection. The first is that of Mr. John Lovett, of the firm of James Lovett & Company. Mr. Lovett was much impressed with the congregation; he had never looked upon such an assembly as he faced in my church. The congregation to him seemed to have the appearance of Joseph's coat, conspicuous for its many colors.

He afterward inquired about this peculiar composition of the audience, and wanted to know if white people were accustomed to attend regularly at the church. I took the opportunity to inform him that the people whom he supposed to be white were not white, but colored, according to the status of the South. "Why," said he, "they are as white as I am." I admitted the truth of his statement, but further explained by saying, that the condition of the colored child usually followed its mother, regardless of the white parentage; that is to say, if the mother was considered colored, the child was considered the same, though the father was white.

This same gentleman was much amused with a little incident that happened while he was present. I had in the pulpit with me a brother minister, who was overcome by the heat and labor of the day, and was inclined to fall in the arms of sweet sleep. At intervals, during my discourse, I would put my hand on this brother and endeavor to arouse him. This seems to have made such an impression on my friend Mr. Lovett, that years afterward, he would joke me about it, and relate the same to his friends.

Mr. Isaac Fenno, who was always thoughtful and kind to me, and assisted me in my work among the freedmen, also visited Richmond during my stay. On the occasion of his visit I happened to preach in the Old African, or better known now, as the First Baptist Church. He was in the audience, but I did not know it until I was through my discourse. When I spied him in the congregation I made haste, like

Zacheus, to come down and shake him by the hand, for I was more than truly glad to see him there, knowing as I did, the deep interest he had in my people. The hand-shake he gave me that morning was valuable as well as warm and sympathetic, for there was left from it a ten-dollar print in my hand. Such handshakes were not unwelcome in those days.

Mr. William B. Spooner, of whom I have spoken before, also made a visit, and because of his special interest and relation to the work among the freedmen, made a good report. Messrs. Walden and Haskell, the well-known tanners of Salem, must also be mentioned as among those who visited Richmond and inspected the nature of the work we were doing.

These gentlemen I have spoken of had more than a personal curiosity in the work I was doing, for they had aided me financially in prosecuting the same; and the visits made fully satisfied them as to the merits and faithfulness of the work.

CHAPTER VIII.

RELIGION AT THE CLOSE OF THE WAR.

I WISH to speak now concerning the general religious status of the colored people at the close of the war, and their relation to their white brethren.

During the heated discussions of slavery and the war conflict, the religious denominations, North and South, divided on the subject of slavery, the northern brethren believing it was wrong to hold slaves, the southern brethren that it was right. The colored people at this time, of course, had no religious rights more than what their masters allowed them. But now by the shock of war they had come into possession of manhood rights, to what wing of the denomination would they ally themselves, to the southern or northern?

At the close of the war, the colored Baptists found that the southern Baptists had formed resolutions against the northern Baptists, and desired to have no communication with them. At the same time the northern brethren were doing much to help the religious life of the colored people. The southern Baptists wanted the colored brethren to ally themselves with them; this the colored brethren hesitated to do, because they considered the northern brethren their friends.

When the proposition was made to us by our white brethren, our reply was, that we would consent on these conditions: *First*, that they would take back all they had claimed and said against the Baptists of the North. And *second*, that they would meet us as Christian brethren, and not as slaves. A meeting was appointed, for both white and colored, to consider the suggestions.

I was appointed by the colored brethren to represent them. And Rev. Mr. Sands, who had preached for the colored people in Manchester, to represent the whites. The said Sands was not only a preacher but a member of the Virginia Bar, a lawyer by profession.

From Slave Cabin to the Pulpit

We met in one of the churches to talk the matter over. His opinion was, that the conditions were too strong.

After we had interchanged views on the subject, we adjourned to meet again at the call of the committee. When the second meeting was called, Rev. Dr. Burrows spoke for the same, and did much to persuade the colored Baptists to affiliate with the white. But as this was the first time in the history of the colored Baptists that we had had to make terms we were inclined to hold to our propositions.

A third meeting was called, in which my old friend, Dr. Jeter, spoke for the white brethren. But this meeting was similar to the other two, as far as the result was concerned, for the colored brethren seemed fully determined as before. Finally, the white brethren abandoned the attempt, feeling, if not expressing it in words, that "Ephraim was joined to his idols," the northern Baptists. The reasons why our white brethren wanted us to affiliate with them, I may not be able to give; certainly, they were very loud in declaring that we had no men who were competent and fit to preach and to act as pastors, but experience has proven the contrary.

I think I voice the sentiment of my brethren when I say, that we chose rather to grope our way in the dark, than to have thrust upon us the kind of preachers we had had in the dark days of slavery, men who could neither sympathize with us, nor preach us the full Gospel. Besides, we knew that our white brethren denied our manhood, and with their own hands had bought and sold human flesh. If we were poor and ignorant we wanted to be consistent.

I recall here an incident that will help to illustrate my meaning. About the time of which I am speaking, a northern missionary by the name of John Vassey, offered Dr. Burrows a Bible as a present. The doctor refused it because of his feeling and attitude toward the North. If the doctor, after having a fair fight with the North, refused the Bible on the ground of consistency, what could he have expected of us, the colored Baptists who hadn't a half of a chance?

At any rate we felt that we were justified in coming out and forming a separate organization.

Accordingly, a convention of the colored Baptists of Richmond and vicinity, was called, for the purpose of considering plans of permanent organization. The meeting convened in the Ebenezer Church, of which I was the pastor, and formed themselves into what is known as the Shiloh Baptist Association of Virginia. Your humble servant was chosen as the first president, and John Oliver, the secretary. The said John Oliver was formerly of Boston, but went South immediately at the close of the war, and rendered much service for his people. I am proud to say that this Association has been productive of much good among the colored Baptists of Virginia.

The question may be asked, how was I treated in Richmond by the local white people during my stay there of nearly five years? In part answer to such a query I would say, that I was treated as well as could be expected under the circumstances. Of course there was a bitter feeling against all persons who hailed from the North, whether they were black or white. And naturally, I came in for my share. Doubtless, a few incidents will better illustrate this point, than I can describe it in language.

On account of the active interest I took in my people, there were some who were inclined to look upon me as a kind of a spy in behalf of the government. Some time after I had relinquished my work and interest in the courts, I was asked one day by a local white gentleman, how much I had received for my service? When I answered him, nothing, he further remarked that "Many of us thought you were a government spy sent here to watch us." It was a duty as well as a pleasure for me to correct this false impression.

I may say here, that once, during my two years' service in the courts, looking after the interests of the colored people, I did receive something; but not from any political source. It happened in this wise: A poor old colored woman had lost her husband by death. The physician who attended him during his illness, sued this poor widow for the house she lived in—which was valued at five hundred dollars. She engaged a lawyer to defend her, but when the case was called the lawyer could not be found. I represented her before the judge, and her house was saved.

This old woman was so pleased and gratified for what I had done, that she brought me two dollars and a half in gold. I refused it, but she insisted that I should take it, or she would be displeased. I took the money; and that is the only compensation that I ever received for my service of two years.

For a while, to say the least, the white South had to endure the presence of the white "Yankees"; but the black or "negger Yankees" they did not want to see, or come in contact with.

Once I called at a lady's residence to see her servant, and while in the kitchen the lady herself came in. And the cook introduced me as the pastor of one of the colored churches, and that I was from the North. She politely recognized me and intimated that she was glad to see me. Then at once she proceeded to speak adversely of the northern people, by saying that they were very mean and stingy, while the southern people were kind and liberal. I remarked, that the northern people had to work hard for their money and they were careful how they used it.

She extended her remarks by saying that she had an "old Anty"— referring to an old colored woman by name—that the "Yankee" had set free; but now she was poor and suffering for the necessities of life. I asked her, about how much money did she think this colored woman to whom she referred, had earned for her during her time of enslavement. "Well," said she, "likely some thousands." This remark caused me to say: "Then, madam, she is entitled to her earnings, is she not?" She expressed herself to the effect that she believed the colored people were made servants for the white people.

I differed with her, and we entered into a discussion of the history of races; she was kind and considerate in her address, and I endeavored to be the same. And thus ended our meeting. I was informed that when her husband came home, she told him that a "negger Yankee" had been in her yard, and about what I had said to her. He expressed himself as being indignant, and regretted that he was not present, so that he might introduce me to the toe of his boot.

Of course I avoided that yard in the future. I must say, however, that I was frequently sent for, by other southern white people, to marry their servants, or preach the funerals.

CHAPTER IX.

A DISTINCTION.

I AM always glad and ready to make the distinction that all white people are not alike. A distinction that many white people are unwilling to make relative to colored people. I do not say, or believe, that because one white man robs a bank and runs away with the people's money, that all white men are thieves and robbers. But the general verdict among white people seems to be that if one colored man steals, all will steal.

There are some white people in the South whom I consider to be very good people, though they were slave owners. Many of them had feelings against slavery, and rejoiced that it was abolished. The opinion of Ex-Governor Henry A. Wise, who hung Brown, will be in place here. I heard Mr. Wise, before Judge Underwood, in the United States Court, make a statement something like the following in substance. While in the course of his argument he turned toward the colored people, and pointing his finger directly at them said, "There is the bone of our contention, and I am glad it is gone, for I knew that slavery and freedom could not exist together in the United States. I tried to get the thing committed to arbitration, and the North, as well as the South, is responsible for its existence, for it was in the original compact, and both sections were a party to it." This utterance of the Ex-Governor of Virginia has always haunted me.

Was the North, as well as the South, responsible for slavery?

This question will doubtless be asked by the generations that are to follow us, and they, more removed from the scenes of conflict, will unhesitatingly give the proper answer. The mills of justice grind slow, but they grind exceedingly fine.

I am glad to admit, also, that a great change has come over the whole country since the close of the war in regard to the opinions concerning the colored people. This is seen in the method of travel,

North and South. In some parts of the North the colored people were denied many of the privileges that they now enjoy.

I remember on one occasion, I was returning to Richmond, from Boston, when arriving at New York, I met the Honorable Frederick Douglass, and we rode together to Philadelphia, where he was to lecture. On our arrival at the depot we took a horse-car for another part of the city. We had boarded the car, Mr. Douglass had taken a seat inside, and I was on the platform. When the conductor got to me, he informed me that I "must get off this car." I asked him why. He replied, he had no argument to make, but "I must get off and take the Jim Crow Car."

I told him that he would have to take the responsibility of putting me off. The conductor, for some reason, had not spied Douglass, seated in the car.

Mr. Douglass at this moment sung out, and wanted to know what was the matter. The aforesaid gentleman was surprised, and exclaimed, "What are you doing out there?" Douglass continued by saying, "Let that man alone; that is Rev. Peter Randolph, from Boston, Massachusetts." "And who are you?" said the conductor, half mad, and thinking that he was contributing something for the amusement of the passengers. The quick reply was, "That is Frederick Douglass."

By this time some of the gentlemen on the car, who had heard the name of Massachusetts, and Frederick Douglass, interfered and told the conductor to let those men alone, that they had no objection to riding with them. The name of Massachusetts seemed to have had a salutary effect in that car, in putting things to right. Long may she live, and hold her place in the front rank of the nation, and exert an influence from ocean to ocean for the oppressed. I believe in that statement which says, the wheels of progress never go backward, but forward.

I have strong faith in the rule of conscience, and I believe that many of the hindrances that now impede the progress of my people will be removed, and that there will be better facilities, and greater opportunities for them.

I regret exceedingly that there are some, who term themselves ministers of the Gospel, who are constantly holding up to public ridicule, the immoral and degraded condition of some colored people, and trying to prove that the colored people as a race are unfit for citizenship. At this writing a prominent minister of New York City, writing on the condition of the colored people, calls them bastards, and says they are immoral and superstitious. It may be that some are without legitimate fathers, and some are immoral and superstitious. But the same may be said of some white people, in almost every thickly-settled community. But would any minister, or anyone else, dare to say all were such? If he did he would be called a lunatic. Before the white South parades the Negro's immorality before the world, let her ask herself and conscience, what has the South done to improve the degraded condition of the colored people. And is she free from all responsibility in this matter? The preacher for the time, should be uncompromising in the truth, not making an apology for sin and wrong-doing, not covering up hypocrisy, but uncovering it, and teaching men the awful consequences of sin. Theodore Parker did not fail to criticise the ministers of the Gospel for neglecting the weightier matters of the law. What we need are more men of his character who are able to arouse public sentiment in behalf of the outraged and the oppressed.

I believe that this age will yet produce brave and noble men who, like Parker, Sumner and Phillips, will champion the cause of the weak and down-trodden, and that they will continue to carry on the glorious work begun by their predecessors.

"Truth crushed to earth shall rise again."

CHAPTER X.

SPECIAL TRAITS.

THE colored people have often been criticised for their emotional and sympathetic traits. I hold that this emotional element is an important adjunct to the progress of humanity. All nationalities have their peculiar traits of character, which, blended with others, add or detract in the great progress of humanity.

The Negro race is deeply sympathetic and emotional, the latter resulting from the former. For where there is deep sympathy, there will be emotion more or less. In the religious worship of the colored people, perhaps, this element of emotion finds its greatest opportunity for display. The Negro is deeply religious, his sympathies run in that direction. He is in full sympathy with religion, and expresses it in his emotions.

Now, this emotional element produces enthusiasm and fires up the cold and indifferent. "More enthusiasm" is what is wanted in all the avenues of life. Then it follows, naturally as the night follows the day, that a deep sympathetic and enthusiastic nature is necessary as a supplement to one that is cold and indifferent.

I admit that some of the demonstrations manifested on the part of many of the colored people in their religious meetings, are not proper—for they are carried to extremes. The meetings carried on till a late hour, the groaning, and shouting, the getting happy, and falling over benches, are features that should be discouraged. All this, doubtless, is the result of a deep religious nature, rough and uncultivated, the overflow of a strong and buoyant spirit. Now, what must be done with this nature? destroy it?

What should be done with a rough and uncultivated, yet productive soil? The iron ore, and the unpolished diamond? Destroy them? The foolish and ignorant could only say destroy them; but wisdom and experience would say cultivate, refine and polish them, and you will have something that will be useful and ornamental. So, in regard to the emotional element in the Negro, cultivate, refine and polish it, and you will have that which maketh not ashamed, but desirable, adding strength and beauty in the great temple of progress.

This sympathetic element is not only seen in the religious worship of the colored people, but also in their daily contact. The Negro is domestic, he loves home, wife and children, and is easily moved to tears by the affliction of any of these. In the dark days of slavery, when parents and children were forced to separate, and that not once, but often, at each separation the scenes of affection were heartrending. I have conducted funerals where it would not be unusual to see nearly the whole adult congregation bathed in tears, while in some white congregations it would be difficult to observe but few, if any, weeping.

Not that the white people do not feel for their beloved dead, but that the manifestation of it does not show itself, as in the case of the Negro.

Often at the graves of their masters, who had whipped and sold them into slavery, the slaves were seen to weep, not tears of joy, but of sympathy and sorrow. This emotional element that is manifested in the Negro's life is usually sincere and without sham or hypocrisy.

Often in the religious meetings, the visitor is caused to smile and laugh out loud, at what appears to him to be amusing, if not ridiculous. But the worshipers, perspiring at every pore, were never more in earnest, and never more sincere. And what is more, this sincerity on the part of the colored people have caused their critics to make allowance for their eccentricities. Now, I maintain, as I have already intimated, that this emotional or enthusiastic element in the colored people—which is natural—is capable of being turned to great good.

To deny the possibility of their development and high state of cultivation, is to deny the current facts of history. Negroes, from the southern plantations and tobacco factories, have stood as representatives in the legislative halls, to champion and defend the rights of man. In all the professions they are found, and when opportunity is given they are ready and able to compete with their more favored brothers for the honors.

The fact that the soil will produce one hill of corn, is an evidence that it will produce another. What man has done, it is reasonable to suppose man can do under similar and favorable circumstances. What, then, must be our conclusion in this matter? This. Encourage the Negro to develop the resources that are within him. He has patience, for he has been the great back-horse and burden-bearer of America. He has sincere faith in God, and enjoys his religion. With his patience, sincerity and enthusiasm he will help to evangelize the world.

After my four years and a half of active service in Richmond and vicinity, I returned again to Boston, my former home. I found on my arrival that a large number of colored people had gathered here from different parts of the South in search of homes and employment. The name Boston always had a musical and joyous sound to the colored people in the South. This was not unreasonable, for this city was foremost in advocating the Negro's cause and vouchsafing to him the immunities of citizenship. May this grand old city always hold the first place in the Negro's affection.

It may be that this fact—Boston's friendship for the Negro—had a little to do with a large number coming to Boston. Be that as it may, the fact is, I found a large number scattered in and about the South End of the city, who were recently from the South. Many of these were like sheep without a Shepherd, leaving their churches in the South behind them, and having no church affiliations here. Owing to the habits and customs in the South, and also their mode of worship, only a few ventured to visit the white churches. I flattered myself as knowing somewhat the needs of my people. After talking the matter over with several brethren, and consulting with my old friend, Deacon Ezekias Chase, I decided to take hold of the work, and do what I could to build up a Baptist Church at the South End.

From Slave Cabin to the Pulpit

Already the good people at Clarendon St. Baptist Church, of which Rev. A. J. Gordon was the honored pastor, had begun work among the children by forming a Sunday School.

This Sunday School, under the auspices of the Clarendon Street folks, was held every Sunday at 1210 Washington Street. I noticed that a number of the parents of these children would occasionally drop in at this school. The thought occurred to me that this was the place to begin a church; accordingly the church was started with a handful of earnest men and women.

All movements, secular and religious, have opposers and obstacles. This struggling branch was no exception to the rule. One of the difficulties I had to contend with during the services in this hall, or place of our first meeting, was the presence of a club of young men in the adjoining apartment. While I was preaching the voices of these men could be audibly heard in my congregation. One would sing out "I pass," another "I have Jack," "trumps," "spades," and such expressions as are common to card players. Doubtless their idea was to get us disgusted, and cause us to leave, that they might continue their gambling on the Lord's day.

We continued to preach, and finally, that peculiar noise of the cards falling on the table ceased, and the young men evidently sat quietly listening to us.

At length they would not gamble at all during the religious service, but would come in, and sit in our audience. Their faces and appearances indicated that they were not the best class of young men. I believe our preaching had a good effect upon them, for when we left the hall for the want of more room, and selected another place of worship, some of these young men continued to visit our services.

During our stay in the hall on Washington Street our numbers were greatly augmented, and we removed from there to the church edifice on West Concord Street, a more commodious place of worship. The latter was secured to us through the kindness of Rev. Geo. C.

Lorimer, D.D., and the dear brethren at the Clarendon Street Baptist Church.

Dr. Lorimer, at this time, was the pastor of the First Baptist Church, located on Shawmut Avenue and Rutland Street. Before we entered the Concord Street meeting-house—which seated about five hundred people—the church was organized and recognized as the Ebenezer Baptist.

I cannot say too much in the way of commendation and praise of the Clarendon Street folks, for their hearty sympathy, cooperation, and financial aid, which was extended to us. Nor too much of the beloved and lamented Deacon Ezekias Chase, who for forty years had been my personal friend. He, with many others, have finished their earthly career, and have gone to receive the reward of the faithful.

At Concord Street our congregation was largely increased, and we had a number of candidates ready for baptism. Unfortunately for us we had no pool in our church, and was compelled to go elsewhere in order to perform the rite. Through the kindness of Dr. Gordon and his officers, our first baptism was observed at the Clarendon Street Baptist Church. According to the arrangements, on a certain Sunday morning, after the doctor's sermon to his congregation, I appeared on the scene with twenty-one candidates, and a large part of my congregation following me. Most of the doctor's congregation had never witnessed what they called a "Colored Baptism", and they remained to see the performance of the same. I have already intimated that most of these people were recently from the South, and their habits and customs were their only heritage from slavery.

I had cautioned them beforehand, that as they were going to Dr. Gordon's church to be baptized, they must be as careful and calm as possible. But I am sorry to say that most of them forgot my advice.

The first one I immersed showed a little sign of excitement, and the second a little more, so the excitement increased gradually, till some got happy in the water, and so on. At the beginning of the excitement Dr. Gordon arose and dismissed his congregation, intimating that it was doubtless best for us to be alone, as we had some ways peculiar to ourselves. He might have added that we had learned these in the house of bondage.

There was one noticeable feature that attracted some attention. As I was baptizing one man, who was quite dark, all at once a voice shouted out in the gallery, "That's my husband." Many of the congregation mistook her for a white woman, but she was a bright mulatto. Rev. Mr. Gordon deeply sympathized with me in my embarrassed condition, and I was so ashamed of the action of my people that I never went there to baptize again.

The Ebenezer Church continued to increase in membership and influence, until to-day it is one of the largest colored churches in Boston. True, the church has had many changes in the pastorate, and this doubtless could not very well be avoided, owing to the composition of the membership and congregation. These were mainly uneducated people, not from one part of the South only, but from different parts. Few had any definite idea of church government, yet all had some idea as to how a Baptist church should be carried on, that is, they thought they did.

Those who came from Virginia had their ideas as to how a church should be conducted, and likewise those who came from North Carolina, Alabama, Georgia or Florida, had theirs also. Each different set wanted their kind of a preacher, and the majority usually carried the day. The uneducated minister would naturally go with the crowd that voted for his coming.

With this peculiar membership the minister would not have smooth sailing all the time. The remedy for this babel state of affairs will come through the intelligent, educated ministry, which shall enlighten the people, and bring them up to the correct standard, and not appeal to their ignorant methods inherited from slavery.

What is needed, also, is more co-operation on the part of the white brethren in this whole matter. This applies to colored churches all over the country. Give the churches better leaders, educated and trained in all doctrine. This the white people must do, for the colored people are poor and have nothing.

Having relieved myself of the work and responsibility of the Ebenezer Baptist Church, I still remained in Boston and vicinity, ready to help in every good work, where my services were wanted. Owing to my relation to the churches and old acquaintance in the city, I was constantly called upon to officiate at funerals, address organizations, and different societies. Frequently I was called to other cities and towns to preach and supply vacant pulpits.

In Providence, R.I., I supplied the Ebenezer Church there for one year, and my stay was blessed with much success. While serving this church I met there some of my relations who were sold from the "Brandon Plantation," on the James River, that I spoke of in the previous chapters. We were unknown to each other, until we found out where we came from. This may seem amusing to some, but it is a common thing among colored people to meet in one another's company for years and not know that they are near kin until some incident occurs like this. In many of the larger cities and towns in the North, and especially in New England, like Providence, Worcester, New Bedford, Springfield, New Haven, Hartford and Newport, there is a large population of colored people, the majority of whom came from the South since the war. They are usually the poorer class of colored people, who come to better their condition; some come direct from the plantations, others from the cities and tobacco factories. As a rule, all are hard-working people, and where they get fair wages and kind treatment they will work themselves nearly to death.

In the South, their great social and religious enjoyment has come through their church life. And naturally they seek such affiliations as soon as they arrive. In many places they are too poor and too few in number to have a self-sustaining church, and ought to remain as a mission under some white church that is willing and able to instruct and assist them.

CHAPTER XI.

IN MANY FIELDS.

SOME of the white Protestant churches have done noble work along this line. The Clarendon Street Baptist Church, of which I spoke, is a good illustration of this fact. But most of the white churches, for some reason, are indifferent or soon tire of the work. The Catholic Church of Rome is taking advantage of this indifference on the part of Protestants toward their colored brother. The progress of the Church of Rome among the colored people for the last few years, will surprise anyone who will look into the subject. The colored people of America in the main, are Protestants, and so inclined. It will be no credit to the Protestant Church of America to let the Church of Rome capture these out of her hands.

It has been my privilege to visit many of these scattered and weak churches, and do what I could to help them.

Worcester, Mass., was also one of the places where I labored for a short time, endeavoring to build up the people.

The colored Baptist here as elsewhere were weak, and struggling for existence. I presented their interest to the white brethren of the denomination, but they were slow to take bold of the work, and rather inclined to criticise the colored people for their mode of worship. This I tried to show was the result of the institution of slavery, for which the whole country was in part responsible.

At the close of my remarks a brother minister arose, and said that he was very much interested in what I had to say. And while continuing he said to the congregation: "Brethren, we may not, as individuals, have injured the colored people, but we have as a nation, and we might just as well acknowledge it." How much better was this simple testimony to the truth than all the skilled and apologetic arguments made in defence of the wrong against the colored people. When Joseph's brethren had time to think and talk the matter over, they said one to the other, "We have wronged our brother." When the American people have had plenty of time to think over their relation to their colored brother, they will make the acknowledgment that the brothers of Joseph made—"We have wronged our brother."

I alluded to the testimony of the minister at Worcester, because it was an exceptional thing for a clergyman to speak out as he did. In the dark days of slavery there was hardly one minister out of a hundred that spoke in behalf of the oppressed slave. And to-day the same might almost be said of the ministers in the South and the North, relative to the barbarous and inhuman outrages committed on the colored people. This is a Christian nation, yet the burning of colored people at the stake is of frequent occurrence.

We tremble and shudder when we read Fox's Book of Martyrs, but who is affected at the burning of Negroes alive in the South? The pulpit should speak out against this blot on American Christian civilization, but it is conspicuous for its silence. We need another Webster to say, "If the pulpit is silent she is false to her trust."

Speaking of the colored people and the difficulties they have in their church affairs, reminds me of a visit I made to Cleveland, Ohio, some years ago. In conversation with the deacon of the First Baptist Church, he turned on this phase of the subject with the colored churches.

He spoke of the difficulties he had experienced in the early history of his own church, and expressed himself as not being surprised at the troubles the colored congregations had; for coming as many of them did, from different parts of the South, uneducated and untrained, confusion was rather expected. This deacon's view is the most intelligent and charitable that I have ever heard from a white brother concerning the colored churches in the North.

His idea on this point is worthy of repetition; certainly if the white churches with all their intelligence and systems have "church fusses", what must be expected where there is no system and no education, to speak of? If the green tree can barely escape, how will the dry tree be effected?

The progress that some of these churches have made in spite of difficulties is an evidence that there are possibilities within the church which, if properly cared for, will make them efficient and self-supporting.

My work at Mashpee, among the Indians, also claims a brief mention in these notes.

Mashpee, Gay Head, and many other settlements in the vicinity of Cape Cod, are distinguished for their Indian descendants. In the early days of New England history, some of the most warlike tribes lived in this neighborhood. Of course, the remnant that now remains is not the genuine article, but a mixture of white and colored people, by intermarriage; still there is much that is characteristic of the Indian. The people at Gay Head and Mashpee have remained somewhat to themselves in a separate reservation, have their own schools and churches, and in the main, they are farmers and fishermen. Some of the best whalers that have chased after the king fish, have come from among these half Indian young men.

The Gay Head boys have made themselves prominent by the bravery that was exhibited in rescuing the survivors from the wrecked steamer, "City of Columbus".

I found the Mashpee people to be kind, intelligent, and lovers of their church, and though my stay among them was of short duration, they were well pleased with the service I rendered them as a preacher.

Their church was located a little back in the woods on a hill, and close by a stream. Tradition says, that this stream or pond, was the favorite trout-fishing ground for Daniel Webster, the great statesman.

While supplying this church I met here a friend of mine from Boston, who was not considered much of a church goer. He expressed the idea that he would like to hear me preach; accordingly, like Nicodemus, he sought a by-path which led indirectly to the church, and sat on the outside to listen while the worshipers were assembled inside. He took his departure, however, before the congregation was dismissed, and no one saw him come or go. He informed some members of the church that he had been to the church and heard me preach, and to convince them, he related a story that I told of a man crossing a river with his sheep, which he characterized as that "sheep story".

The last time I met him in Boston he wanted to know about that old "sheep story". As I was the first colored preacher to supply these people, they turned out en mass on the first Sunday, and manifested much curiosity, expecting to see me get happy, jump up and shout. Happily for them, they were forced to change their minds in this respect.

Nantucket, which seems to be cut off from the rest of the world, cannot be reached by the pedestrian; but he who would reach its shores must go by the way of the briny deep. I had made arrangements to supply the Baptist Church on this island for a short time, but the Sunday I was expected, I did not arrive, because there was so much water between myself and the island. It has been the rule of my life always to be punctual in regard to my appointments, and doubtless much of the success I have had is due to this fact; but this is one of the times that I "got left".

I had been misdirected as to the direct course to Nantucket, and after going a station or two out of my way, I had to return and start again, and accordingly, when I arrived at Hyannis on the Cape, where I was to take the steamer, the boat not waiting for me, had taken its departure, and there would not be another until Monday morning. I was informed, also, that the next train back to Boston, would be on Monday morning—this was anything but consolation.

From Slave Cabin to the Pulpit

I was at two extremes, the end of the railroad and at my wits' end. Here I found myself in a strange place and among strange people, and must remain half the day Saturday, and all day Sunday. What to do was the question?

I inquired for the Baptist pastor and found one, Rev, J. Brownston by name. He met me at his door as a gentleman and a Christian. I related to him my story and disappointment in not reaching Nantucket. He extended to me the hospitalities of his home, and invited me to remain over Sunday. I attended the service in his church in the morning; the theme of his discourse was the providence of God in the affairs of men.

He referred to me as an illustration of the subject. How, in the providence of God, I was prevented from going to Nantucket, that I might remain in Hyannis over Sunday. The subject and the manner in which he treated it, made a great impression upon me. He announced to his congregation that I would preach in the evening, and give some account of my slave life and advent to Boston. Accordingly, at the evening service a large congregation was present. I did the best I could in way of preaching, and related some facts of my slave life. How I came to Boston in 1847, with sixty-six companions, and so on.

One of the pleasant and surprising things to me was, that there was an old brother in the audience who remembered the time of our arrival, and was one among the crowd that greeted us at Long Wharf, Boston. The presence of this gentleman gave a double emphasis to all I had to say on this point.

On Monday morning I took my departure from Hyannis, believing firmer than ever, that the providence of God guides in the affairs of men. In crossing that part of the Atlantic that lies between Nantucket and the main land, one must not look for all smooth sailing, if so, doubtless there will be some disappointment, but you must be willing to smell and taste a little of "old Ocean".

From Slave Cabin to the Pulpit

On reaching Nantucket I was much impressed with the place and its people, though the first impression was not a very favorable one, for I was looking for a larger town and more activity among the people. It was certainly a sea-girt island, and ancient in its architectural structures. The people were of a mixed population, with much of the Indian element, whose main occupation was that of fishing.

In the early days of whale-fishery Nantucket was one of the leading ports. The people are proud of their history, and take great delight in showing strangers dilapidated buildings, that are distinguished for their age.

The traditional history of the name Nantucket, seems to be quite familiar among the young people. They will tell you about the three islands the sovereign of England gave to his three daughters, Martha, Elizabeth and Nancy.

The first two were taken by Martha and Elizabeth, and called respectively, Martha's Vineyard, and Elizabeth Islands. As there was only one left, "Nan," she took it; and the island bears the name of Nantucket, because Nancy took it. I cannot say positively that Nancy got the best of the three islands, for when I discovered that I had to eat clams or fast—knowing that I was not too fond of that fish—I desired to be in a more convenient place. On the whole, my stay at Nantucket was pleasant and I have made several visits to the island.

I will also briefly state, that I preached for a while in Albany, New York. And also served the church at West Newton, Mass., for one year. All these fields I have mentioned include the time after my return from the South. Doubtless much of the work done in these fields was imperfect. But I have had occasion to rejoice again and again at the result of the seed that was sown.

CHAPTER XII.

THE LAW.

AS I was born a slave in the South and deprived of all educational advantages, the opportunity for self-improvement, after my emancipation, I rarely allowed to go by, though I had a family to support. When I was pastor in New Haven I availed myself of the public lectures that were given. Also in like manner, when I was in Richmond, Va., I attended the school for preachers there, and I always sought the presence and companionship of those who were able to help me, through the conversation and discussion of important subjects.

Accordingly, soon after I gave up the active pastorate of the Ebenezer Baptist Church, Boston, I entered the law office of E.G. Walker, Esq., and read law for a while, not with a view of practicing but for the sake of a more definite idea of the common law. With this general knowledge I thought I could render much acceptable service to many of my people who are ignorant of their environments and the laws that govern them.

I was made a justice of the Peace, under Governor Washburn, and reappointed by Governor Long and Governor Ames, respectively. While in this capacity I rendered helpful service to some of my people. But as this was not my calling I did not continue in it very long.

Before closing these brief but important sketches of my life, from slavery to freedom, I wish to relate a pleasant episode that happened on one of my return visits from Richmond to Boston.

Owing to the ill health of my wife and family, it was necessary for me to make stated visits to the North, at the same time availing myself of the opportunity of informing and interesting my friends in the southern work. During one of these visits I happened in the Boston Post Office one day, and on entering, my eyes rested on what appeared to be a flat pocket-book; I examined the contents and found the name of Charles Vinell attached.

I inquired of the delivery clerk if he knew of such a person; he informed me that the said Vinell had called for letters and that he resided down on Cape Cod. I was acquainted with one Deacon Vinell who lived in Cambridge, Mass., and had his office with Gardiner Colby. Accordingly I called on Mr. Vinell, told him my story of the pocket-book, and asked him if he knew this Mr. Vinell, from the Cape. He informed me that he often did business with him, and that he was a distant relative of his.

In the meantime Mr. Vinell, the owner of the pocket-book, was exercising himself not a little in search of his property.

He had visited five different places to see if he had left it "there". His agitation of mind can better be imagined than described; doubtless he scratched his head more than once where it did not itch, endeavoring to stir up his memory, for that wallet contained what might be regarded by some as a small fortune. Finally he found his way back to the Post Office, which at that time was located on State Street. As he entered, full of excitement, the clerk anticipated him by saying, "You have lost your pocket-book, sir?" He intimated he had, and that he had been hunting everywhere he had gone, for it, and wanted to know if anyone had seen it in the office.

The Post Office clerk assured him that the purse had been found, and was safe in the hands of a colored man whom he knew, the Rev. Peter Randolph, who was preaching among the freedmen in the South, and that he could be found at the office of Gardiner Colby. He forthwith struck a B-line for this office, where I happened to be at the time. As he entered some one said to me, "That is Mr. Vinell." As he came in, with his face radiant with a smile, I approached him and said, "You have lost your pocketbook, sir?" He seemed too full for utterance, and gave only smiles for answer. As I returned the pocket-book I asked him how much it contained. "Something over five thousand dollars," was the reply. As he received it, he said, "Now, what shall I give you?" "Anything you please, sir." He gave me five dollars and an invitation to visit him at his home on the Cape.

A few days after this I read in the papers that a colored boy from Richmond, Va., had picked up a purse of five thousand dollars, and was liberally rewarded with five dollars. This newspaper article gave two impressions that I wanted to correct; the first was, that I was not a boy, but a man, considered old enough to vote, if nothing else. So accordingly I called on Mr. Haskill, editor of the Transcript, and related to him the correct story relative to the pocket-book.

He published the same in his paper and informed the public that I was not the boy spoken of, but the Rev. Peter Randolph, who was pastor of a large church in Richmond. The second impression I wanted corrected, was that I was not complaining because of what Mr. Vinell gave me, for I considered him the only rightful possessor of the purse and contents. When my many friends learned that I was the person who had found the money, they came together and presented me with a present of some two hundred dollars.

I accepted Mr. Vinell's invitation and made him a visit at the Cape, which was very pleasant and profitable, and through his influence I was able to solicit the sympathy and co-operation of several friends in the southern work.

If there is any moral to this pocket-book story, it is this: Honesty is always the best policy, and brings its own reward.

CHAPTER XIII.

RETROSPECT.

THE river has its bend and the longest road must terminate. As I look backward and take a retrospective view of my past toils and sorrows, and the vicissitudes through which I have passed, I feel that I have much to be thankful for. I am greatful to Almighty God for emancipation from cruel southern bondage, and for directing my course to liberty-loving Massachusetts. I am thankful to that noble band of men and women who, by pen and tongue acting under the highest impulse, did not hesitate to perform their duty in behalf of outraged and oppressed humanity.

I shall never forget those brave and patriotic men who, tearing themselves from the embrace of their families, hastened to the scene of conflict and poured out their dearest blood for freedom and right.

I thank God for the unity and good feeling that exist between the North and South; for the material prosperity of which we have a right to boast; and join with others in the grand anthems of praise:

"My country, 'tis of thee, Sweet land of liberty," "God bless our native land," and, "Firm may she ever stand."

But, with all my gratitude and praise, I still feel ashamed of the present condition of our colored Americans, in this great country.

A candid review of that condition will show that it is far from what it ought to be, in view of the great loss of blood and treasure.

The sacrifices and insults that the anti-slavery folks were forced to endure, the suffering and privations of the soldiers on the battle-field, and in prison pens; the loss of over a million lives, and eight billions of money, should have been sufficient to dig a grave so deep for slavery, that it would never rise again to vex the country in any form.

From Slave Cabin to the Pulpit

Doubtless there are many who think this has been done, and done once for all. I sincerely hope so.

But, as in the days of slavery, so now, I hear the voice of my oppressed brethren in the South, crying for help and protection. Protection from the lash, shot-gun, lynching, and that most fiendish custom—which was unknown in the days of slavery—the burning of colored people alive at the stake. These, my outraged brethren, have again and again waited upon the President through their delegations, and presented to him their grievances, The delegations have been politely received, only to be informed that the President could do nothing. They have returned to their homes to be abused the more for daring to complain of the treatment accorded them by the white South.

Outrageous methods are resorted to, in order to defraud the poor people out of their honest toil, and deprive them of their civil and political rights. Many of these methods are known to both white and colored.

If the colored citizens dare to come together and defend themselves and their homes, the attacking party raise the cry of "Race Riot", and forthwith the state militia hurries to the scene to shoot and abuse the colored people only.

White men who condemn and speak out against this condition of affairs are gagged, or forced to leave the section for a more congenial clime. The pulpit and press, which are recognized forces in every community, encourage, rather than condemn, the persecution of the colored people; the pulpit by its silence, the press by actually urging it on.

A colored man may be arrested on suspicion of crime, and before his trial or even he reaches jail, the southern press publishes to the world, that "a black fiend has been arrested, and it is likely he will be lynched."

From Slave Cabin to the Pulpit

The white South seems to think the colored Americans have but few rights that they are bound to respect, and they have the colored people in their hands, as clay in the hands of the potter, to mould into shape, or dash into pieces. The North—judging from its indifference and non-interference—are gradually turning the whole "Negro question" over to the South to take care of.

What will the South do with the Negro? will be the question. Will she educate and elevate him as an intelligent citizen or degrade him to a serf and slave? She has the power to do either.

The unconditional control the victorious North permitted the conquered South to exercise over the colored people since emancipation, is one of the things that will perplex the future historian for explanation. The North, with the aid of two hundred thousand colored soldiers, succeeded in giving the South a severe thrashing. President Lincoln, when he saw the bravery and courage that was displayed by these soldiers on the battle-field—regardless of his previous opinions he may have held on the subject—declared before his God, that the four millions of slaves in this country should be free. And General Benjamin F. Butler, when he rode over that memorable battle-field and saw the ground covered with brave black soldiers, then and there, he resolved before God, "To these people ever to be true." And he kept his word to the letter; and when he breathed his last at the national capital his colored friend and faithful servant was the last one to look upon his living countenance.

Lincoln and Butler had good reasons for changing their former views relative to the status of the colored people in this country.

Their position to the general government, and to their former masters, should have guaranteed to them better protection.

To set them free, and leave them without the necessary protection, at the mercy of their former owners, maddened by reason of their defeat, was indeed an oversight.

From Slave Cabin to the Pulpit

The southern whites could forgive their northern brethren for taking up arms against them; but for the colored man and slave who dared to take up arms against the South, there could be no forgiveness; the only thing for them was death.

And they have endeavored to make the Negro's freedom taste as bitter to him as the dregs of slavery ever tasted.

Charles Sumner, with the insight of a true statesman, anticipated this state of affairs. Realizing as he did, that the Negro question was directly or indirectly the source of all the trouble, it was his supreme desire and aim, to so fix this question once for all, that unlike Bancho's Ghost, it would never arise to frighten the American people again. He said to the country in acts, if not in words, the only way to settle this question, is to change the status of the Negro, make him a man with all the rights of an American citizen, and put in his hands the ballot as a means of his protection. He labored for the realization of this result, but died before its consummation.

Among his last words were these: "Do not forget my Civil Rights Bill."

The North has forgotten it, and the South has thrown it overboard as a "blunder of statesmanship".

I shall never forget my interview with Mr. Sumner at the Coolidge House, Boston, on one of my return visits from the South.

The object of my visit was to lay before him the condition of my people as I viewed them, from personal contact.

It was early morning when I called, about the time he was to have his breakfast. As I was ushered into his presence, he remarked that I would have to talk to him while he was eating, for his time was so taken up that he had but few moments to spare.

I began by saying, that there was never a people in all the history of the world, that were placed in a similar position as my people are placed at the present time.

I spoke of the madness of the slaveholders as analogous to that of Pharoah when he was forced to let the people go. "But," I continued, "the Red Sea separated Pharoah and his slaves; the freedmen of the South were left with their masters where there was hate and malace indescribable. The subject of the king departed with gold, silver, and herds of cattle; but the poor emancipated slave had nothing but his empty hands." As I thus began to talk with Senator Sumner, he rested his knife and fork, and looked at me with signs of deep sympathy. Said he:

"Mr. Randolph, in my feelings and sympathies, I am a colored man, and feel most deeply all the wrongs that your people suffer."

He also referred to the trouble he was having with his own party; intimating that it was departing from its true principles, and about to leave the colored man out in the cold.

Many of us have been taught by experience that Sumner was right, and this will be seen more and more as the years advance.

If Sumner was wrong in advocating the ballot for the Negro, Lincoln was wrong in issuing his emancipation proclamation; if the proclamation was a "military necessity", the ballot was a necessity, for in the absence of military protection, the ballot was the only protector. To condemn one is to condemn the other.

Freedom and the right of franchise have come to the colored man through the terrible ordeal of war. The question that is paramount to all questions is: Shall the results of the war be recognized? This question the North must ask herself, and put it to the South, and demand an answer. Nowhere in our broad land—North or South—are freedom and citizenship accorded to colored people as to others.

From Slave Cabin to the Pulpit

There are not a few who endeavor to excuse their treatment of the Negro, because of his vices. They say he is a thief, unreliable and immoral. To intimate that all men are thieves and liars, because one man is found out to be so, is to manifest one's ignorance of human nature; which is the same in a black man as it is in a white man, under similar circumstances.

To say that all colored people are dishonest and of a bad character, is to be guilty of the same foolishness.

On examination it will be found that the honesty and integrity of the colored people will compare favorably with others in the community. Those who are dishonest and immoral are greatly indebted to the institution of slavery, for their inheritance.

Slavery taught them to steal food, by depriving them of sufficient food. It taught them to lie, by punishing them severely when detected, and taught them to be immoral by compelling men and women to marry again and again, after their husbands and wives had been sold, that they may raise a new set of children for the slave market. Also, by the forced relation of some of the masters and slave-drivers, who begot children by slave women, and sold the females at a high price to become mistresses for white men.

When our southern friends speak of the immorality of the colored people, without giving the cause, they should have their fingers guarded upon their lips.

Regardless of all these signs of discouragement there are still signs of encouragement. The progress the colored people have made in face of all difficulties is phenomenal.

Since their emancipation they have increased from four millions to eight millions. Every seat in their schoolhouses is filled, and there is an urgent appeal for more efficient schools. The colored population in the United States pay taxes on $264,000,000 worth of property.

And according to Mr. Grady's statement, the colored people in Georgia alone pay taxes on forty million dollars ($40,000,000) worth of property; and according to the auditor's last report of Virginia, they pay over twelve million dollars ($12,000,000) on taxable property.

The colored man is not only a plantation hand, but he is a mechanic, tradesman and banker; he is a preacher, teacher, editor, lawyer and doctor. The colored people in the States support seven colleges, seventeen academies and fifty high schools, in which there are thirty thousand pupils.

They have one million, five hundred thousand children in the common schools, and twenty-four thousand teachers. More than two million, five hundred thousand of the race can read and write.

To let the Negro alone, remove all impediments out of his way and encourage him to make progress along these lines, will solve what appears to many to be a difficult problem.

The duty of the colored man for the hour is to prepare himself to be an intelligent and industrious American citizen.

The white people of this country and of the world should be patient with the Negro in his progress, for it will be impossible for him to eliminate in one generation the evil effects of two hundred and fifty years of American slavery.

Christian civilization, if it has free course, will adjust difficulties. If this cannot, what will? Will emigration solve the question? No, that will simply throw our duty and responsibility on others.

Will extermination satisfy? No, it will add insult to injury, and like Cain and his brother, will greatly add sorrow to this life and the life to come. There is but one rule, and one only, that can solve the "Race Problem," and all difficult problems.

That rule came from Heaven through Jesus Christ, and was given to man as his only safe guide; It is called the Golden Rule: "Do unto others as you would have others do unto you." On this rests the joy or sorrow of America.

CHAPTER XIV.

SOME OF MY FRIENDS.

IT is an old saying but a true one, that he who would have friends must show himself friendly.

These are the names of some of my friends who have manifested their friendship during the changing scenes of my life, in addition to those mentioned in the Second Chapter:

Frederick Batcheller,
Geo. E. Batcheller,
W. Patton,
L. Patton,
Chas. Morey,
A. Safford,
Samuel James,
F. Baker,
H. M. Moon,
F. J. Smith,
John Rand,
Pliny Smith,
A. Pratt,
R. Goodwin,
W. E. James,
J. D. Lovett,
Peter Hobert,
Ezekias Chase, Jr.,
Chas. Wiggins,
Chas. Wiggins, Jr.,
K. R. Tolman,
O. Holmes,
P. C. Johnson,
F. Nazro,
Walter Smith,
Wm. Butler,

Geo. Denney,
E. W. Wheelock,
Ralph Warner,
Wm. C. Bond,
J. H. Clinch,
Wm. F. Mullen,
Hugh Carey,
Geo. Freeman,
Geo. Simmons,
Edward Kinnard,
Henry Callender, Jr.,
John Bishop,
Frederick Mosley,
Flavell Mosley,
Rev. A. J. Gordon, D.D.,
Rev. A. A. Miner, D.D.,
Rev. O. P. Gifford, D.D.,
Rev. Geo. C. Lorimer, D.D.,
John C. Lovell,
William Butler,
Cumming Bray,
John Hitchcock,
Wm. C. Durant,
Wm. Cole,
Chas. Cole,
Matthew Cox,
Chas. L. Andrews,
Author Hebbert,
F. Moody,
J. M. Clinch,
Wm. Newton,
Nathaniel Comner,
Nathaniel Jones,
Samuel Loud,
O. V. Brown,
Dr. Samuel Birmingham,
Mrs. John Lorthop,
Samuel Hatch,

Mr. Cudwell,
Samuel Hodgman,
Wm. Harris,
Chas. Roundy,
Chas. Cheney,
J. C. Bishop,
N.C. Bray,
W. E. Crocker,
H. G. Hotchkiss,
A. Van Wagnor,
J. Kendall,
Wm. Wardwell,
James Baxter,
Miss R. Bates,
Joseph Toctman,
Geo. R. Kelso,
Geo. Cooper,
J. A. Chebut,
Benj. Lovell,
Amos Thompson,
W. J. Converse,
Lucius Cheney,
Messrs. Rhodes and Ripley,
Geo. R. Eager,
Miss Hattie Eager,
Miss Fannie Eager,
E. Thayer,
J. Sawyer,
C. Boynton,
Mr. Thompson,
Dea. Hill,
John May,
Chas. Butler,
Joseph Tuttle,
Mr. Lovejoy,
Mr. Frost,
Matthew Boles,
Paul Deen,

From Slave Cabin to the Pulpit

Geo. Chipman,
Chas. Phipps,
J. Roberts,
Jno. L. Patch,
Henry Prunk,
C. Mash,
Mr. Edmons,
O. H. Simson,
Chas. H. Newt,
Jno. R. Davis,
Wm. Taylor,
J. Manning,
Henry W. Comner,
Chas. Barrett,
Chas. Smith,
Mr. Griffis,
Mr. Hewes,
John Daniels,
Chas. Daniels,
Noble Hill,
Mr. Dadford,
Mr. Priest,
Amos Tapley,
Mr. How,
Silas Lothrop,
Willis Van Wagner,
Samuel Noyes,
J. C. Cambell,
Jno. M. Williams,
Mrs. Sarah Bond,
Richard Bond,
Wm. Claflin,
Mr. Vinson,
Walter B. Hewins,
Henry Jenkins,
O. J. C. Benn,
Wilson Owens,
Samuel Johnson,

E. R. Morse,
O. M. Wentworth,
Geo. T. Clark,
O. A. Door,
J. Brown,
Alexander Vaughn,
Frank Hinkley,
Moses A. Noyes,
Jno. D. Manning,
C. A. Mudge,
Geo. Robinson,
Nathaniel How,
Geo. Dexter,
Jno. Brigham,
Wm. B. Nye,
Ira B. Orcutt,
Frank Loring,
Mr Lyons,
Mr. Vose,
Edward Potter,
J. Moor,
Abner Tower,
Moses Tower,
Moses Tower, Jr.,
Geo. Callender,
Messrs. Hartshorn and Hunt,
Wm. L. Garrison,
Wendell Phillips,
Wm. C. Humphres,
F. O. Dewey,
Wm. Varney,
Walter N. Dole,
Albert E. Prince,
A. S. Moore,
S. S. Weston,
Wm. H. Dunbar,
S. Stilman Blanchard,
Ezra Farnsworth,

Levi L. Wilcott,
Wm. Lincoln,
R. D. Green,
A. Demmick,
S. G. Bowdler,
A. Skilton,
Riley Pebles,
Geo. Blake,
Mr. Brown,

SKETCHES OF SLAVE LIFE

INTRODUCTORY NOTE TO SKETCHES OF SLAVE LIFE.

IT was on the morning of the 15th of September, 1847, that I learned from a constant and true friend to the slave—Mr. Robert R. Crosby—that a large company of colored people, said to be emancipated slaves from Virginia, were then landing from a schooner at Long Wharf. I immediately went thither, and found the report correct. The people in question were in part upon the wharf, and some had not yet left the vessel. I entered into conversation with several of their number, and learned that they had been slaves in Prince George County, Virginia, on the estate of Mr. Carter H. Edloe, on the James River. Mr. Edloe died in 1844, and by will provided for the emancipation of his slaves, and for the payment to each one of fifty dollars, whenever they should elect to receive their freedom and go out of the State of Virginia. With a few of his slaves, for especial reasons, he had dealt much more liberally. The provisions of Mr. Edloe's will, it would appear, however, were not carried out in the spirit of the testator, and there is reason to believe that the executor designedly deceived and wronged the slaves. They were kept at work upon the estate as slaves for more than three years after their master's death, on the pretence that there was not money sufficient to pay them the sum which the will specified. At the end of that time, in despair of obtaining their rights under the will, the larger part of the people determined to take what they could get, which was *less than fifteen dollars each*, and go to a free state. There were sixty-six of them—of both sexes and of all ages, from seventy-five years down to infancy—who decided to go to Boston. Their passage was secured in the schooner Thomas H. Thompson, Wickson, master, by which vessel they arrived in Boston, as stated above.

Such was the story told to me; and I may add, that further inquiries have entirely satisfied me of its correctness. I found these emancipated people without exception, desirous of obtaining situations where they might at once go to work— none fearing but that they could support themselves and their families, if they could find employment. Of course I expressed my readiness to aid them in obtaining places, if they wished to do so. The offer was gratefully accepted, and without much loss of time, places were found, out of the city, for about one half of them. The remainder found homes and occupation in the city, or its immediate vicinity.

Eight years have now nearly elapsed, during which time I have observed the course of these emancipated slaves with attention and with some curiosity. I regarded the experiment they were making as an exceedingly interesting one as, if successful, ought to convince even the most skeptical, of the ability of the colored man, even when reared in the ignorance and partial dependence which the condition of slavery imposes, to "take care of himself". For this was not a company of slaves selected for any special capacity, or of such as by their own skill and daring had achieved freedom. They were the ordinary working force of one plantation—of all ages and capacities, and in various states of health; and might be presumed to be a fair representation of the average condition, at least, of Virginia slaves. The experiment—if any choose so to regard it—has had a fair trial, and has resulted, I can truly say, very much to their credit. Since the first few months after their arrival—when, on account of their destitution and the strangeness of a new home, occasional help was needed by a number of them—the instances in which they have sought charitable aid have been few and infrequent. Even an aged and nearly worn-out man of their number for six years maintained himself by his daily labor, and only ceased to attempt it longer, when told that he must desist by reason of infirmity of age, at upwards of four score years. Generally, so far as my knowledge extends, they have secured for themselves a sufficient though frugal living, and some of them have decidedly prospered. And in regard to sobriety, honesty, and general good conduct, they will not suffer by comparison with any like number of people in the community.

It affords me a sincere pleasure to be able to give this testimony in behalf of these people, our hardly-treated brethren. For, unusually fortunate as they were in having a master so eccentric as to believe that his slaves desired liberty and were entitled to it, yet their lot in slavery left, as it ever must, on body and mind, indelible marks of its blighting power. When all the untoward, disheartening, soul-crushing influences of their former life are considered, it seems to me not less surprising than it is honorable to themselves, that they have used their liberty so justly and so well.

I think it well to subjoin their names and ages, from a list taken by me at the time of their arrival. Some of them have gone "where the wicked cease from troubling, and the weary are at rest."

LUCY FOUNTIN, 76.

CHAS. FOUNTIN, ab't 40.

WM. FOUNTIN, do.

CARTER SELDEN, 47,
wife and six children.

LEVI SCOTT, about 75.

DANIEL — —.

PETER RANDOLPH, 27,
wife and child.

ANTHONY RANDOLPH, 24.

RICHARD RANDOLPH, 22.

JAMES RANDOLPH, 10.

WYATT LEE, 25,
wife and two children.

FRANK CHURCHWELL, 54.

ADAM HARRISON, 55.

GEORGE MAYERSON, 45,
wife and two children.

BURRY ROBESON,
wife and two children.

DAVY MEAD, 45.

PATTY MEAD, his wife.

TORRINGTON RUFFIN, 36,
wife and four children.

WILLIAM ARCHY, 32,
wife and five children.

DAVY JONES, 40.

ANDREW CLARK, 23,
wife and child.

HENRY CARTER, and wife.

AMY RICHARDSON, 29,
two children.

JUDY GRIFFIN, 26,
two children.

FANNY BAILEY, 30.

SAM. JONES, 24.

RICHARD WHITING.

JACK HARRISON, 29.

RALPH WEBB, 24.

PETER TAYLOR, 36.

The unpretending work, written by one of the above *sixty-six*, is commended to the public as wholly trustworthy, and deserving of their favor.

SAMUEL MAY, JR.

CHAPTER I.

THE SYSTEM.

THE good anti-slavery men have very much to contend with, in their exertions for the cause of freedom. Many people will not believe their statements; call them unreasonable and fanatical. Some call them ignorant deceivers, who have never been out of their own home, and yet pretend to a knowledge of what is going on a thousand miles from them. Many call them dangerous members of society, sowing discord and distrust where there should be nought but peace and brotherly love. My Readers! give attention to the simple words of one who knows what he utters is truth; who is no stranger to the *beauties* of slavery or the *generosity* of the slaveholder. Spend a few moments in reading his statement in regard to the system of American slavery. Do not scoff or doubt. He writes what he does know, what he has seen and experienced; for he has been, for twenty-seven years of his life, a slave; and he here solemnly pledges himself to TRUTH. Not once has he exaggerated, for he could not; the half of the woes and horrors of slavery, his feeble pen could not portray.

This system is one of robbery and cruel wrong, from beginning to end. It robs men and women of their liberty, lives, property, affections, and virtue, as the following pages will show. It is not only a source of misery to those in bonds, but those who fasten the chains are made wretched by it; for a state of war constantly exists between the master and servant. The one would enforce obedience to his every wish, however wrong and unjust; he would exact all the earnings of the slave, to the uttermost farthing. The latter feels the restraint and writhes under it; he sees the injustice, and at times attempts to assert his rights; but he must submit either to the command or the lash; obey implicitly he must.

The argument so often brought forward, that it would be for the interest of the owner to treat his slaves well, and of course he would not injure his own interests, may do for some, but not for the thinking and considerate. When does the angry tyrant reflect upon what, in the end, will be the best for him? To gratify his passion for the moment, to wreak out his revenge upon a helpless menial, is, at the time of excitement, his interest, and he will serve it well.

Many argue that the southern masters are not to blame for this wrong; they inherited it from their fathers, it is said, and what can they do? Get rid of it! Would it be sensible to suppose that generation after generation were justifiable in becoming drunkards, because some ancestor had been? Certainly not; any person who reasoned thus would be considered insane. If my father stole, or murdered, would that excuse me for committing the same crimes? No; we all know better than that.

Again, it is said, the slaveholder has bought them and paid his money for them; perhaps his whole property is in them; should he give them up, and beggar himself? If his property consists in human beings, surely he should give it up, though he starved in consequence. Of whom has he bought them? Who can own humanity but the great Creator? As the good Vermont Judge said—"Show a bill of sale from the Almighty, and we acknowledge your claim."

Some will say, "The slaveholder cannot live without the Negro; the climate will not permit the white man to toil there." Very well; admit it. Then let him grant to men their rights; make them free citizens; pay them justly for their honest toil and see the consequences. All would be happier and better. Slavery enriches not the mind, heart or soil, where it abides; it curses and blights everything it comes in contact with. Away, away with, tear up by the roots, these noxious weeds, which choke the growth of all fair plants, and sow in their stead the beauteous flowers of freedom, well watered by the pure waters of religion, and what a rich harvest will be yours!

CHAPTER II.

SLAVES ON THE PLANTATION.

THE slave goes to his work when he sees the daybreak in the morning, and works until dark at night. The slaves have their food carried to them in the field; they have one half hour to eat it in, in the winter, and one hour in the summer. Their time for eating is about eight, in the morning, and one in the afternoon. Sometimes, they have not so much time given to them. The overseer stands by them until they have eaten, and then he orders them to work.

The slaves return to their huts at night, make their little fires, and lie down until they are awakened for another day of toil. No beds are given them to sleep on; if they have any, they find them themselves. The women and men all have to work on the farms together; they must fare alike in slavery. Husbands and wives must see all that happens to each other, and witness the sufferings of each. They must see their children polluted, without the power to prevent it.

HOW THE SLAVES CONTRIVE TO GET FOOD.

There are some animals in Virginia called raccoons, possums, old hares, and squirrels. The best of these is the possum, which lives in old trees and in the earth. The slave sets his trap in the swamps where the possum usually lives. The traps are made by cutting down trees, and cutting them in short pieces about five feet long; then they raise the log on three pieces of stick, like the figure four. These traps are made on the Sabbath. One slave will sometimes have fifteen or twenty of them, and will go at night, with his torch of pitch-pine, and see if his traps have caught anything for him to eat. Sometimes he finds a possum and a raccoon; and sometimes a squirrel and old hare. This old hare is something like a rabbit. All of these animals are good food for the poor slave, and make him feel very glad that he has them to eat. Some of the slaves hunt these animals with dogs, trained for the purpose They run them up the trees in the forest, where, as they are a harmless animal, they can be taken very easily.

They do not fight very hard when caught, but are very easily overcome; but they are a deceitful little animal. They will lie on the ground, and make you think they are dead; but if you leave them, they will creep off so soon, that you cannot conceive how the little animal got away so cute. The only way they can be kept safely is to be put in a bag, or in a basket with a cover. The slave knows best when to hunt these creatures. The best time is just at the rise of the tide in the rivers. There is another method that the slave takes to get his food. He makes what is called a fish trap. This is made by cutting white oak wood into very small strips, which are tied together with a great deal of ingenuity. This trap is put in very deep water, and attended by the slaves at night, and on the Sabbath (this being all the time they have to attend to their traps); and very glad are they of this opportunity, of getting some nice fish. Often-times the overseer will take what he wants for his own use, and the slaves must submit.

There are some little fruits in Virginia, that are called "simmons"; they grow very plentifully, and are sweet and good. The slaves get them in the fall of the year, then they get a barrel and put the "simmons" into it, and put water there too, and something else that grows on trees, that they call $locusses", which are about ten inches long, and two across. They put the "locusses" and "simmons" into the water together, and let them stand for two or three days. Then the water is drained off, and the leaves are used as you would use coffee. The slaves put this liquid in gourds, and carry it to the field with them, and drink out of their gourds while they eat their bread.

HOUSE SLAVES.

When the slave-master owns a great many slaves, ten or a dozen are always employed to wait on himself and family. They are not treated so cruelly as the field slaves; they are better fed and wear better clothing, because the master and his family always expect to have strangers visit them, and they want their servants to look well. These slaves eat from their master's table, wear broadcloth and calico; they wear ruffled-bosomed shirts, too—such as Doctor Nehemiah Adams declares he saw while on his visit to the South, where he became so much in love with the "peculiar institution". These slaves, although dressed and fed better than others, have to suffer alike with those whose outward condition is worse. They are much to be compared to galvanized watches, which shine and resemble gold, but are far from being the true metal; so with these slaves who wait upon their masters at table—their broadcloth and calico look fine, but you may examine their persons, and find many a lash upon their flesh. They are sure of their whippings, and are sold the same as others.

Sometimes their masters change, and put them on the farm, that the overseers may whip them. Among those who wait upon the master, there is always one to watch the others, and report them to him. This slave is treated as well as his master, because it is for the master's interest that he does this. This slave he always carries with him when he visits the North; particularly such slaves as cannot be made to leave their master, because they are their master's watch-dog at home. So master can trust them. Before leaving, master always talks very kindly to them, and promises something very great for a present, if they are true to him until his return.

These slaves know what they must say when asked as to their treatment at home, and of the treatment of their fellows. They leave their wives, their mothers, brothers and sisters, and children, toiling and being driven and whipped by the overseer, and tortured and insulted on every occasion.

DECEPTION OF THE SLAVEHOLDER.

All the slaves, as well as their owners, are addicted to drinking; so when the slaveholder wants to make a show of his "niggers" (as he calls them), he gives them rum to drink.

When the master knows a northern man is to visit him, he gives orders to the overseer, and the overseer orders every slave to dress himself, and appear on the field. If the slaves have any best, they must put it on. Perhaps a man has worked hard, extra times all the year, and got his wife a fourpenny gown—she must put it on, and go to the field to work. About the time the stranger is expected, a jug of rum is sent to the field, and every slave has just enough given him to make him act as if he was crazy.

When such a stranger as Rev. Dr. Adams appears with the master, he does not see the Negroes, but the rum that is in them; and when he hears their hurrah, and sees their Jim-Crow actions, he takes it for granted that they are as happy as need be, and their condition could not be bettered.

The owner gives the visitor liberty to ask his "niggers" questions. He will ask them if they love their master, or wish to leave him. Poor slave will say, he would not leave his master for the world; but oh, my reader! just let the poor slave get off, and he would be in Canada very soon, where the slaveholder dare not venture.

The slaves do not speak for themselves. The slave-holding master and his rum are working in their heads, speaking for slavery; and this is the way the slaveholder deceives his friend from the North.

FLOGGING.

For whipping the slaves in Virginia, there are no rules. The slave receives from the slaveholder from fifty to five hundred lashes. The slave-owner would think fifty stripes an insult to the slave. If the slave is let off with fifty lashes, he must show a very good temper. Men, women and children must be whipped alike on their bare backs, it being considered an honor to whip them over their clothes. The slaves are placed in a certain position when they are flogged, with sufficient management to hold them very still, so they cannot work their hands or feet, while they are "wooding them up," as they call it in Virginia.

Some of the slaves have to lie down on their stomachs, flat on the ground, and be stretched out so as to keep their skin tight for the lash, and thus lie until they receive as much as they choose to put on; if they move, they must receive so many lashes extra. When the slaveholder expects to give his slave five hundred lashes, he gives him about half at a time; then he washes him down with salt and water, and gives him the remainder of what he is to have. At such times, the slave-owner has his different liquors to drink, while he is engaged in draining the blood of the slave. So he continues to drink his rum and whip his victim. When he does not flog his victims on the ground, they are tied by their hands, and swung up to a great tree, just so the ends of their toes may touch the ground. In this way, they receive what number of lashes they are destined to. The master has straw brought, that the blood may not touch his shoes. Ah, reader! this is true, every word of it. The poor slave is whipped till the blood runs down to the earth, and then he must work all day, cold or hot, from week's end to week's end. There are hundreds of slaves who change their skins nearly as often as they have a new suit of clothes.

CHAPTER III.

FARMS ADJOINING EDLOE'S PLANTATION.

I WILL give my readers a little knowledge concerning the neighbors of my owner, that they may be able to judge of slavery by something more than the character of one slaveholder, or his management among his slaves.

Edloe's farm was what was called Upper Brandon, on James River. It consisted of about fifty-six square miles, and was worked by eighty-one slaves.

William B. Harrison owned Middle Brandon. His farm was about one hundred square miles. He owned over two hundred slaves. Of their treatment I shall speak, and also of the numerous overseers he had employed.

George B. Harrison, the owner of my father, owned Lower Brandon. His farm was the same in size as his brother's and he owned the same number of slaves.

William B. Harrison fed his slaves what is called "regular" in Virginia; he was one of the best feeders on James River. He clothed them well, too; but he was a great flogger, and probably the greatest in the region. In his dealings with those who were not slaves, he was upright, never deceiving, but always doing as he agreed. If any other case than slavery came before him, he would make a liberal decision in favor of right; but he would have his slaves whipped whenever the overseer wished it. Sometimes he would go to church and preach to his slaves. I have heard him myself, but, my readers, it did seem like mocking God for such as he to stand up and preach.

The first overseer of Mr. Harrison's that I knew was Benj. Bishop. Under his reign, many of the slaves went into the presence of their God, to show the bloody stripes of the lash received from Ben. Bishop. Harrison did not care for his slaves as the man who owned me did, but left them to the mercy of the overseers. Go to the South, reader! there you will see many mulattoes, the descendants of Ben. Bishop. He continued with Harrison several years, when, being sent down to Richmond to sell some Negroes, he made one hundred dollars more than he was to pay his employer; therefore, he concluded to take the business of human traffic into his own hands, and become a "nigger trader". He was not very successful in his undertaking, being too fond of what is called "toddy" in the Southern States. He became a great drunkard and a great gambler (vices intimately connected with the "peculiar institution"), and was obliged to give up his business.

He was afterward employed by Edloe, my master; but he did not live with him long before he was discharged, for his unmerciful treatment of the blacks.

Death called to him soon, and he was ushered into the awful presence of the righteous judge (who listens to the cries of the poor widows, and the orphans), with his guilty hands dripping with the blood of his fellow-creatures, who had sunk groaning to the earth beneath his barbed heel of cruel oppression.

The next man who took charge of this farm was John Q. Adams. This man (notwithstanding his noble name) was a disgrace to civilization; for when he had beaten his victims till their bodies could bear no more, he would lash the bottoms of their feet. My readers, this may seem incredible, but it is truth. Harrison's slaves trembled at the very mention of his name, and the sight of him would bring woe and terror to their very souls; the poor creatures would wish that the earth would open and swallow them, that they might never look upon the face of Adams again, or hear the sound of his voice. His voice had all the fearful sound of the roaring lion, and the hideous howl of the prowling wolf. I verily believe his organs of speech were made of the hardest granite, fastened together with monstrous iron bolts. As his victims were dripping with their own blood, he would bellow forth his curses, and dare them to call on God for help. Groanings and sorrow, pains and misery untold, unspeakable, were the portion of the Negroes upon Harrison's plantation.

Adams practised everything that was mean, cruel, devilish, everything that could be thought of by demons. This conduct continued eleven years before I left Virginia, in 1847. I could give a great many more truths concerning this J. Q. Adams, that may seem too outrageous for a human being to conceive. I would not do injustice to anyone, not even a slave-driver, for I know I must stand at the bar of the Eternal, and render an account of every word spoken in the flesh. I know that, in order to do good, my testimony *must be the truth.*

The next overseer was Harden Harrison. He owned three slaves himself; but was very religious, and belonged to the Presbyterian Church. He did not beat so much as Adams, but was very strict with the slaves. He used to say his prayers every night, and grace before his meals. Sometimes his grace failed him, and then the poor slave must expect something more than soft words or gentle treatment. He never yet had grace sufficient to excuse any little fault in a Negro. He used to quote Moses' law to whip by. His face was very narrow and hypocritical.

He had just enough of professed religion to deceive. He was one of those calculated to deceive northern visitors, who saw him go on with his solemn ceremonies of religion, to make them believe that good and religious men guided the poor ignorant blacks, and kept them from sinking entirely into the blackness of heathenism. Then Mr. Harrison would take just enough of his toddy to make him feel as good as anybody else. He lived with Mr. W. B. Harrison as long as he wished, then left and went home to his own farm.

The next overseer was named Edloe. He used to call himself the "snapping-turtle", and would raw-hide the slaves so they would be obliged to wind cotton around their persons, to protect their wounds from their clothing. Of other things of which he was guilty, delicacy forbids me to speak; judge for yourselves. He continued there three years, and was at it when I left Virginia.

One more of these men I have not mentioned, whose name was Ladd. It should have been "Hornet". I cannot speak of the actions of this man, without a shrinking from the fact that I ever knew such a being. He made men and women to growl and bark like dogs. At all hours of the night, you might find Ladd in the woods, with his dogs, prowling about after some skulking fugitive, and all day driving and whipping the persecuted victims, till they were almost driven to self-murder, which nothing but the belief that those who take their own lives cannot be happy in another world kept them from. The slaves used to run away to Edloe, and get him to go and beg mercy for them, and he would do so. For two years, Ladd managed in this way; then the great Judge called him from earth, to give an account of his bloody deeds.

Some of my readers may ask why we were always afflicted with such horrid men, as overseers, in our region, and if there were no good ones. Ah, dear reader, do you think a good man would take such a position? And what man is there who would not become worse daily by being placed in such a situation, with unlimited power over hundreds of abject beings whom he looks upon as only a little above the brute? Ah, ye who look coolly on in the distance, and doubt the existence of all this wretchedness, go nearer, become yourself the property of another, and then your doubts will be removed!

The first overseer I knew of on George Harrison's plantation was Charles Charbour. "Devilish" is the only word which will describe his character. My father was a colored driver under him, and he was made to beat his fellow slaves most unmercifully, and there was no escape, unless he would have submitted to a worse fate, if possible, for himself. Charbour has been known to cut the skin with a knife from the poor black man's feet, that he might not run away, or that the saying, "I will cut off ever inch of your black hide," might be literally fulfilled. Truly, he was one toward whom the blood of the slave will cry, whenever he approaches those fields of labor, or wanders by the swamps, or by the riverside. There was no peace for man, woman or child, wherever he followed.

Harrison, who owned the slaves, was a young man at this time, and cared for nothing, so Charbour had everything his own way. God in his mercy visited this farm with a great calamity. The cholera came among the slaves, and carried many to their rest. The very atmosphere, at this time, seemed to burn with evil and wrong for the poor Negroes, so that death was their best friend. Many of my father's relations were owned here, and well we knew of the sufferings which their owner allowed, and sought no means to alleviate.

Harrison's conduct at last made him an object of scorn and indignation to most of the people who knew him. One day, he was on business at the court house, and while he was seated among many gentlemen, who were strangers to him, they commenced a conversation about "young Harrison", and his abominable course in regard to his people. Very freely they discussed his character, and he had the benefit of their opinion from their own mouths. He went home rather humbled, and commenced the work of reformation on his plantation. Charbour was forbidden to whip so much, and the slaves were really treated better. That season was to the slaves what the conversion of Paul was to the church he had persecuted—there was rest for a little season. Shortly after this sudden change in Geo. Harrison, he died, when the clouds of darkness again fell about those poor Negroes. His brother became the guardian of the estate, and everything was left in the hands of overseers, who used their power as bad men might be expected to.

Another neighbor of ours, or rather, of my master's, was his brother. His plantation was called Willow Hill, and was very large. This Mr. Edloe owned two farms (one in Cumberland Co.), and a great many slaves. Many of these slaves were related to me, and those of my fellows who came North with me.

William Allen owned a large farm across from Lower Brandon, in Surrey Co., called Claremont. He also owned twelve other farms, and nine hundred and ninety-nine slaves. He was uncle to Edloe, my owner, and was considered the richest man in Virginia, except old Bob Bolling, of Petersburg. He was not a good man. He was possessed of none of the virtues but some of the vices of King Solomon. He was very fond of the young females, yet he was married to no *one*. He was very cruel to his people, and used what is called the bell and horns on his slaves, to keep them from running away. He used to chain them together with a long chain, with heavy fastenings at the end of the chain. The bell and horns were a harness made so as to fasten on the slave's neck, with a band of iron that would go round the neck, to which was attached another band that passed over the top of the head, about three feet perpendicular, then turned with a hook, so as to hook over the limbs of trees, if the slave should attempt running in the swamps, out of sight of the overseer. He always kept a good stock of them on hand, to use as you would use bells for cows, that you might find them easily, if they strayed.

Some of his slaves were put to death by his overseers, but he did not trouble himself about it—he had plenty more. Ah, my readers! more blood has been drawn from Allen's slaves than he would be willing to carry upon his shoulders for one moment.

He was very close with his slaves with regard to food and clothes, and those who lived along the rivers used to catch fish at stolen moments, so as to keep themselves along, from time to time, until Allen died. When that occurred, Edloe immediately went over, and freed all the poor creatures from their harnesses, leg-irons, and handcuffs. Allen had freed his colored sons, and about eight others. The rest of his slaves he gave to one of his nephews, named William Allen. He gave one of his farms to be divided among all his relations. Edloe was one, and he drew eighteen of those slaves, who were all freed with myself. The rest went to drudge with their new masters, under a bondage worse than Egyptian.

CABIN POINT.

There was but one village near Brandon, where the large farms were cultivated, and that was in Surrey County, about seven miles from Lower Brandon. This village was called "Cabin Point", and there the United States mail stopped. Five or six stores were kept there, and it was a great place for loafers; for at these stores you could buy almost everything, especially rum and other liquors. Saturdays and Sundays, all the lower class of whites and free colored people used to assemble there, to drink and gamble. No slaves were allowed there, unless sent by their masters, with a pass.

"Cabin Point" was famous for its fighting, drunkenness, and every kind of degradation. The whites beat the free colored people there, and they dare not raise their hands, lest they should be mobbed. Females were not safe there an instant; nothing could protect them from the violence of those drunken desperadoes. If any good man from the North should witness one of these scenes, he would think it indicative of anything but civilization.

This place was the rendezvous for all the rowdies of Prince George and Surrey Counties. There the overseers would meet for their drunken revels, and return to the farms, to make the backs of the outraged Negroes pay the bills for their debauchery.

There were many wealthy men there, who owned many human beings. The most prominent among them were Mr. Peters, A. Sledge, Dr. Strong, and Dr. Graves.

Dr. Graves was so cruel and wicked, he would not take time even to whip his slaves, but would use his knife on them. He would chain them on their backs, and give them nothing to eat for two or three days at a time. He was called the best physician in the place, but he was as good a devil as I should wish to see. He was employed by all the large farmers to attend their slaves in sickness, and was very fond of the female slaves, to whom he was a good doctor. I will not spend time to write more of him; he was so wicked, my feelings become excited, and language fails me in speaking of him.

Dr. Strong was a mild man—as fine a man as I ever knew among slave-holders. He was not cruel; he looked upon his Negroes as human beings, possessed of feelings, and as capable of enjoyment and suffering as himself, and he treated them kindly He appeared to be a Christian; but still, he held his fellow-men in bondage; he did not allow them to act for themselves and work for themselves. Even kind-hearted Dr. Strong could not live out the precepts of Jesus and remain a slave-holder. He was succeeded by Dr. Gray, who, though a very strict man among his people, was not cruel.

Mr. Peters was not as bad as many other slaveholders, though he used to whip his slaves to keep them tame, for fear they would run wild. Mr. Peters was a mild whipping slave-holder, died a slave-holder, and will receive a slave-holder's reward.

Amos Sledge was very cruel and inhuman in the treatment of his people. He worked them very hard, fed them very poorly, clothed them but scantily, whipped them unmercifully, and allowed them no privileges. They were a downcast, heartbroken set of people.

CHAPTER IV.
OVERSEERS.

THE first overseer I served under was Henry Hallingwork, a cruel and a bad man. He often whipped my mother and the children, and worked the slaves almost day and night, in all weather. The men had no comfort with their wives, for any of the latter who pleased him, he would take from their husbands, and use himself. If any refused his lewd embraces, he treated them with the utmost barbarity. At night, he watched the slaves' huts, to find out if they said anything against him, or had any food except what he had allowed them; and if he discovered anything he disliked, they were severely whipped. He continued this conduct for about three years, when Mr. Edloe discovered it, and discharged him.

The next overseer who lived on the plantation did not treat the people so badly as did Hallingwork, but he drove them very hard, and watched them very closely, to see that they took nothing but their allowance. He only lived there two years, when he was discharged for misconduct.

The next overseer, a man named Harris, only remained about six months; his cruelty was so great, it came to Mr. Edloe's ear, and he was discharged.

The successor of Harris was L. Hobbs. He was very cruel to the people, especially to all women who would not submit to him. He used to bind women hand and foot, and whip them until the blood ran down to the earth, and then wash them down in salt and water, and keep them tied all day, when Edloe was not at home. He used to take my cousin and tie her up and whip her so she could not lie down to rest at night until her back got well. All this was done on Edloe's plantation, the good *slave-holder* who owned me; and the other slaveholders used to say to him that he "spoiled his niggers"; but this was the way he spoiled them. Hobbs continued this ill-treatment for the space of three years, then he was turned off. Thus ends the history of Hobbs on Edloe's plantation, with the exception of leaving what are termed "mulattoes" in Virginia.

The fifth overseer was B. F. Bishop. He came to the plantation as a tyrant, and proved himself such to men, women and children. He reigned tyrannically for one year, and did many things which decency will not permit me to speak of. He, and all of the overseers, were in the habit of stealing from their employer, and the colored people knew it, but their informing Edloe would have done no good, for he could not believe a slave. According to the laws of Virginia, the testimony of a slave against an overseer could not be taken. This Benj. Bishop reigned "monarch of all he surveyed" (doing as he chose in everything—cruel as cruel could be) one year, when he was discharged.

The sixth overseer was R. Lacy, a native of Charles City, Va. He reigned seven years. I cannot describe to my readers the malice and madness with which this being treated Edloe's slaves. You cannot find his parallel in history, except it be in Nero or Caligula. Indeed he was a very wicked man, and a hypocrite. I cannot point to one good deed he ever performed. He would enter the houses, and bind men and women, and inflict torture upon them, whether innocent or guilty. The blood of innocent slaves is yet crying, to the God of justice to avenge their sufferings, and pour out deserved judgment upon the head of Lacy.

The seventh overseer was P. Vaughn. He was cruel, but not so much so as some of the others had been. He was too fond of rum and the females, so Edloe gave him his walking ticket.

The eighth overseer was J. G. Harrison. He was with Mr. Edloe at the time of his decease. Harrison was, like others in his station, hard and unmerciful. He made his dogs tear and bite my mother very badly. She died soon after, and was freed from her tormentors, at rest from her labors, and rejoicing in heaven.

This same Harrison shot one of Edloe's men, because be would not submit to the lash; but no one said anything to Harrison about his conduct. (He did not kill the man. Although shot, he is now living in Charlestown, Mass. His name is Wyatt Lee. He is well known in Boston.)

FOOD AND CLOTHING.

I shall now show what the slaves have to eat and wear. They have one pair of shoes for the year; if these are worn out in two months, they get no more that year, but must go barefooted the rest of the year, through cold and heat. The shoes are very poor ones, made by one of the slaves, and do not last more than two or three months. One pair of stockings is allowed them for the year; when these are gone, they have no more, although it is cold in Virginia for five months. They have one suit of clothes for the year. This is very poor indeed, and made by the slaves themselves on the plantation. It will not last more than three months, and then the poor slave gets no more from the slave-holder, if he go naked. This suit consists of one shirt, one pair of pants, one pair of socks, one pair of shoes, and no vest at all. The slave has a hat given him once in two years; when this is worn out, he gets no more from the slave-holder, but must go bareheaded till he can get one somewhere else. Perhaps the slave will get him a skin of some kind, and make him a hat.

The food of the slaves is this: every Saturday night, they receive two pounds of bacon, and one peck and a half of corn meal, to last the men through the week. The women have one half pound of meat, and one peck of meal, and the children one half peck each. When this is gone, they can have no more till the end of the week. This is very little food for the slaves. They have to beg when they can; when they cannot, they must suffer. They are not allowed to go off the plantation; if they do and are caught, they are whipped very severely, and what they have begged is taken from them.

CHAPTER V.

CUSTOMS OF THE SLAVES, WHEN ONE OF THEIR NUMBER DIES.

THEY go to the overseer, and obtain leave to sit up all night with their dead, and sing and pray. This is a very solemn season. First, one sings and another prays, and this they continue every night until the dead body is buried. One of the slaves makes the coffin—and a very bad one it generally is. Some wheat straw is put in the coffin, and if they can get it, they wrap the body in a piece of white cloth; if they cannot get it, they put the body in the coffin without anything around it. Then they nail up the coffin, and put it in a cart, which is drawn by oxen or mules, and carried to the grave. As they have no tombs, they put all the slaves in the earth. If the slave who died was a Christian, the rest of the Christians among them feel very glad, and thank God that brother Charles, or brother Ned, or sister Betsey, is at last free, and gone home to heaven—where bondage is never known. Some, who are left behind, cry and grieve that they, too, cannot die, and throw off their yoke of slavery, and join the company of the brother or sister who has just gone.

When the overseer is in good humor, he will let all the people go to look the last time upon their relative; if he is ill-tempered, he will not let the slaves go at all; so it all depends upon the state of mind the overseer is in, whether the child is permitted to look upon the remains of its parent, the husband upon his wife, the mother upon her child, or any other dear relative. Ah, my readers! think of this, and see the cruelty of the "peculiar institution". Slaves have tender human feelings—very warm and tender they are; but it matters not how sorrowful and heavy a heart the poor Negro may have, he cannot see his lifeless friends unless the slave-holder wills it.

When several of the slaves die together, the others go to their owner, and ask him to let them have a funeral. Most of the owners will grant their slaves this privilege. When the owner and overseer give their consent, the slave-holder sends a note to a white preacher; then they set the day, and the slaves make ready for the funeral services over their friends.

The slaves go to the woods, and make seats to sit upon (this is done Saturday night). When the seats are prepared, they are left till the slaves take their seats upon them, and sit until about ten o'clock, when the slave-holding minister comes, and preaches about one hour and a half. Then he gives the Negroes liberty to sing and pray, and he stands by them. This is to keep the slaves from their master, because they are not allowed to meet together, except a white man be present. At the funeral, all the slaves from the adjoining plantations obtain passes from their overseers, and come; so this is really a great day for the poor blacks to see each other. If their hearts are sad, they are happy to see their friends, and they all go to some place, and their friends receive such entertainment as it is in their power to give. They stay together till night draws on, and then each leaves for his home. As soon as possible after the funeral, the slaves must go to their work. They have no person to speak a word of comfort to them, to cheer their heavy hearts; but they must go on working and mourning all the day and night. If they had some one to sympathize with them, their burden would be light; but no one cares for the tears of the widow, the sighs of the disconsolate husband, the sobbing cries of the mother, whose little son or daughter has been taken from her. No one pities the widow's son, that his mother (who labored all her life for the slave-holder, and for her son, when she could get an opportunity) is gone to the grave, leaving her only one behind, to toil on yet longer beneath the lash of tyrant overseers, and at the mercy of unfeeling slave-holders. Ah, my readers! even in the grave there is more comfort to the sad ones afflicted, than in the prison-house of hopeless slavery. Once, oh, northern reader, visit the auction-block, and all that is human within your soul will be aroused, and you will feel and know *what American slavery is.*

CHAPTER VI.

SLAVES ON THE AUCTION-BLOCK.

THE auctioneer is crying the slave to the highest bidder. "Gentlemen, here is a very fine boy for sale. He is worth twelve hundred dollars. His name is Emanuel. He belongs to Deacon William Harrison, who wants to sell him because his overseer don't like him. How much, gentlemen—how much for this boy? He's a fine, hearty nigger. Bid up, bid up, gentlemen; he must be sold." Some come up to look at him, pull open his mouth to examine his teeth, and see if they are good. Poor fellow! he is handled and examined like any piece of merchandise; but he must bear it. Neither tongue nor hand, nor any other member, is his own—why should he attempt to use another's property?

Again the bidder goes on: "I will give one thousand dollars for that boy." The auctioneer says, "Sir, he is worth twelve hundred at the lowest. Bid up, gentlemen, bid up; going, going—are you all done?—once, twice, three times—all done? GONE!"

See the slave-holder, who has just bought the image of God, come to his victim, and take possession of him. Poor Emanuel must go away from his wife, never to see her again. All the ties of love are severed; the declaration of the Almighty, which said, "What God hath joined together, let not man put asunder," is unheeded, and he must leave all to follow his *Christian* master, a member of the Episcopal Church—a partaker, from time to time, of the Lord's Sacrament. Such men mock religion and insult God. Oh, that God would rend the heavens and appear unto these heartless men!

Next comes Jenny and her five children. Her husband was sold and gone. The oldest of her children is a girl seventeen years old—her name, Lucy.

Auctioneer—"Here, gentlemen, is a fine girl for sale: how much for her? Gentlemen, she will be a fortune for anyone who buys her who wants to raise niggers. Bid up, gentlemen, bid up! Fine girl; very hearty; good health; only seventeen years old; she's worth fifteen hundred dollars to anyone who wants to raise niggers. Here's her mother; she's had nine children; the rest of them are sold. How much, gentlemen—how much? Bid up! bid up!"

Poor Lucy is sold away from all the loved ones, and goes to receive the worst of insults from her cruel task-master. Her poor mother stands by heart-broken, with tears streaming down her face. Oh! is there a heart, not all brutish, that can witness such a scene without falling to the earth with shame, that the rights of his fellow-creatures are so basely trampled upon? The seller or buyer of a human being, for purposes of slavery, is not human, and has no right to the name.

The next "article" sold is Harry, a boy of fifteen.

Auctioneer—"Gentlemen, how much for this boy? He is an honest boy, can be trusted with anything you wish; how much for him?"

Harry is sold from his mother, who is standing for her turn. She began to scream out, "Oh, my child! my child!" Here the old slaveholder said, "Ah, my girl! if you do not stop that hollering, I will give you something to holler for." Poor Jenny, the mother, tried to suppress her grief, but all in vain. Harry was gone, and the children cried out, "Good-by, Harry; good-by!" The broken-hearted mother sobbed forth, "Farewell, my boy; try to meet me in heaven."

The next of the children was Mary. She was put upon the block and sold. Then the mother became so affected that she seemed like one crazy. So the old rough slave-holder went to the mother, and began to lay the lash upon her; but it mattered not to her—her little Mary was gone, and now her turn had come. Oh, mothers who sit in your comfortable homes, surrounded by your happy children, think of the poor slave mother, robbed so cruelly of her all, by a fate worse than death! Oh, think of her, pray for her, toil for her, ever; teach your blooming daughters to think with compassion of their far-off colored sisters, and train them up antislavery women! Teach your sons the woes and burning wrongs of slavery; make them grow up earnest, hard-working anti-slavery men. When mothers all do this, we may hope yet to live in a *free country.*

Wretched, childless, widowed Jenny was placed upon the block for sale.

Auctioneer—"Gentlemen, here is Jenny—how much for her? She can do good work. Now, gentlemen, her master says he believes her to be a Christian, a very pious old woman; and she will keep everything straight around her. You may depend on her. She will neither lie nor steal: what she says may be believed. Just let her *pray*, and she will keep right."

Here Jesus Christ was sold to the highest bidder; sold in Jenny to keep her honest, to bring gold to the slave-holder. Jenny was sold away from all her little children, never to see them again. Poor mother! who had toiled day and night to raise her little children, feeling all a mother's affection for them, she must see them no more in this world! She feels like mourning—"like Rachel weeping for her children, and would not be comforted, because they were not." So she commends them to the care of the God of the widow and the fatherless, by bathing her bosom in tears, and giving them the last affectionate embrace, with the advice to meet her in heaven. Oh, the tears of the poor slave that are in bottles, to be poured out upon his blood-stained nation, as soon as the cup of wrath of the almighty Avenger is full, when he shall say, "I have heard the groanings of my people, and I will deliver them from the oppressor!"

Slave-holders carry the price of blood upon their backs and in their pockets; the very bread they eat is the price of blood; the houses they live in are bought with blood; all the education they have is paid for by the blood and sorrow of the poor slaves.

In parting with their friends at the auction-block, the poor blacks have the anticipation of meeting them again in the heavenly Canaan, and sing—

"O, fare you well, O, fare you well!
God bless you until we meet again;
Hope to meet you in heaven, to part no more.
CHORUS—Sisters, fare you well; sisters, fare you well;
God Almighty bless you, until we meet again."

Among the slaves there is a great amount of talent, given by the hand of Inspiration; talent, too, which if cultivated, would be of great benefit to the world of mankind. If these large minds are kept sealed up, so that they cannot answer the end for which they were made, somebody must answer for it on the great day of account. Oh, think of this, my readers! Think of that day when it shall be said to all the world, "Give an account of thy stewardship!" Among the slaves may be found talents, which, if improved, would be instrumental in carrying the blessed Gospel of Truth to distant lands, and in bringing the people to acknowledge the true and living God. But all has been crushed down by a Christian world, and by the Christian Church. With these solemn facts written against this nation, see to it, my readers, before this iniquity overthrow you, and it be too late to repent.

The sin of holding slaves is not only against one nation, but against the whole world, because we are here to do one another good, in treating each other well; and this is to be done by having right ideas of God and his religion. But this privilege is denied to three millions and a half of the people of this, our own "free" land. The slaveholders say we have not a true knowledge of religion; but the great Teacher said, when he came on his mission, "The Spirit of the Lord is upon me, because he hath anointed me to preach the Gospel to the poor. He hath sent me to heal the broken-hearted; to preach deliverance to the captive, and recovering of sight to the blind; to set at liberty them that are bruised, and to preach the acceptable year of the Lord." This ought to be the work of the ministers and the churches. Anything short of this is not the true religion of Jesus.

This is the great commandment of the New Testament—"Love the Lord thy God with all thy heart, and thy neighbor as thyself." "Do unto others as ye would that they should do to you," is the golden rule for all men to follow. By this rule shall all men be judged. We have got to hear, "Come, ye blessed; depart, ye cursed!" These are my convictions, and my belief of the religion of Jesus, the wonderful Counsellor of the children of the created Adam, our great progenitor.

In view of these things, I earnestly beg my readers to renew their interest in the anti-slavery cause, never turning a deaf ear to the pleadings of the poor slave, or to those who speak, however feebly, for him. The anti-slavery cause is the cause of HUMANITY, the cause of RELIGION, the cause of God!

CHAPTER VII.

CITY AND TOWN SLAVES.

THE slaves in the cities (Petersburg, Richmond and Norfolk, in Virginia) do not fare so hard as on the plantations, where they have farming work to do. Most of the town and city slaves are hired out, to bring in money to their owners. They often have the privilege of hiring themselves out, by paying their owners so much, at stated times—say once a week, or once a month. Many of them are employed in factories and work at trades. They do very well, for if they are industrious, they can earn considerably more than is exacted of them by their owners. All can dress well, have comfortable homes, and many can read and write. Many of them lay up money to purchase either their own freedom or that of some dear one. These slaves are not subjected to the lash as the poor creatures upon the plantations are, for their owners would feel (as every man should feel, in the true sense) their dignity fallen, their nobility sullied, by raising the whip over their human property.

Slavery, as seen here by the casual observer, might be supposed not to be so hard as one would imagine, after all the outcry of philanthropists, who "sit in their chimney-corners amid the northern hills, and conjure up demoniac shapes and fiendish spirits, bearing the name of slave-holders." But slavery is *slavery*, wherever it is found. Dress it up as you may, in the city or on the plantation, the human being must feel that which binds him to another's will. Be the fetters of silk, or hemp, or iron, all alike warp the mind and goad the soul.

The city slave may escape the evil eye and cruel lash of the overseer, but if he offend the all-important master, there is retribution for him. "Hand this note to Captain Heart," (of Norfolk), or "Captain Thwing," (of Petersburg)—and well does the shrinking slave know what is to follow. These last-mentioned gentlemen *give* their time to, and improve their talents by, laying the lash upon the naked backs of men and women!

Ah, my dear readers! take what side you will of slavery—Dr. Adams' "South side", or the Abolitionist's North side—there is but *one side*, and that is dark, *dark*. You may think you see bright spots, but look at the surroundings of those spots, and you will see nothing but gloom and darkness. While toiling industriously, and living with a dear family in comparative comfort and happiness, the city slave (whose lot is thought to be so easy) suddenly finds himself upon the auction-block, knocked down to the highest bidder, and carried far and forever from those dearer to him than life; a beloved wife, and tender, helpless children are all bereft, in a moment, of husband, father and protector, by a fate worse than death;—and for what? To gratify some spirit of revenge, or add to the weight of the already well-filled purse of some *Christian white man*, who professes ownership in his fellow-man. Wretch! you may command, for a season, the bones and sinews of that brother, so infinitely your superior; but, remember! that form is animated by a never-dying spirit! it will not always slumber! A God of infinite love and justice reigns over all, and beholds your unholy, inhuman traffic! Believe you, justice will triumph, the guilty shall not go unpunished on the earth! the righteous are to be recompensed, *much more the wicked and the sinner.*

The whipping-posts are the monuments of the religion and greatness of the southern cities, though none but the basest of men officiate there; yet they think as much of their office as a poor conceited dandy would of his, were he raised to the Presidency of some great institution.

Yet with the knowledge of all these wrongs constantly thrust before the people, they willfully shut their eyes, and will not see; and thousands who walk these shores, free men, support by word and deed this abominable wickedness! Yes, even the ministers of our religion defend, from those temples erected for the worship of the one living and true God, this "domestic institution!" With all their official sanctity, they enter the sacred desk, dedicated to the service of a God of tender mercies, and consecrated to the work of imparting to those congregated before it the teachings of that pure and holy One, who preached deliverance to the captives, and opened the eyes of the blind, who rebuked sin wherever found— among rulers or servants, in the synagogues, the halls of justice, or by the public ways—and, instead of imitating their Divine Master, the American clergy uphold these crying enormities of the "dear people", who feed and pamper their luxurious appetites, and clothe them in fine linen. Ah, my readers! I was once a slave, and was a partaker and witness of all its horrors till I was twenty-seven years old. I, in my ignorance, felt that I was called of God to preach His acceptable word to this downtrodden race. Through his mercy, I was made a *free man*, and now resolve to devote my life, my all, to the spreading of the truth in regard to this great sin of our nation. And Oh! it makes my heart ache, when I see and hear those men, possessed, all their lives, of every advantage, receiving their education at our seats of learning stand up before the people, as lights of the world and defend the slave-holder, or forever hold their peace in regard to the plague-spot of slavery.

What right, human or divine, can one man have to another, who, like himself, was created in the glorious image of our common Father and Creator? How can such men pray, *"Our Father"*? How can they talk about the human family, and the great day of judgment which is to come? Surely, like the false prophets of old, they are deceiving the people.

CHAPTER XIII.

RELIGIOUS INSTRUCTION.

MANY say the Negroes receive religious education—that Sabbath worship is instituted for them as for others, and were it not for slavery, they would die in their sins—that really, the institution of slavery is a benevolent missionary enterprise. Yes, they are preached to, and I will give my readers some faint glimpses of these preachers, and their doctrines and practices.

In Prince George County there were two meeting-houses intended for public worship. Both were occupied by the Baptist denomination. These houses were built by William and George Harrison, brothers. Mr. G. Harrison's was built on the line of his brother's farm, that their slaves might go there on the Sabbath and receive instruction, such as slaveholding ministers would give. The prominent preaching to the slaves was, "'Servants, obey your masters'. Do not *steal* or *lie*, for this is very wrong. Such conduct is sinning against the Holy Ghost, *and is base ingratitude to your kind masters, who feed, clothe and protect you.*" All Gospel, my readers! It was great policy to build a church for the *"dear slave"*, and allow him the wondrous privilege of such holy instruction! Edloe's slaves sometimes obtained the consent of Harrison to listen to the Sabbath teachings so generously dealt out to his servants. Shame! shame! to take upon yourselves the name of Christ, with all that blackness of heart. I should think, when making such statements, the slave-holders would feel the rebuke of the Apostle, and fall down and be carried out from the face of day, as were Ananias and Sapphira, when they betrayed the trust committed to them, or refused to bear true testimony in regard to that trust.

There was another church, about fourteen miles from the one just mentioned. It was called "Brandon's church", and there the white Baptists worshiped. Edloe's slaves sometimes went there. The colored people had a very small place allotted them to sit in, so they used to get as near the window as they could to hear the preacher talk to his congregation. But sometimes, while the preacher was exhorting to obedience, some of those outside would be selling refreshments, cake, candy and rum, and others would be horse-racing. This was the way, my readers, the Word of God was delivered and received in Prince George County. The Gospel was so mixed with slavery, that the people could see no beauty in it, and feel no reverence for it.

There was one Brother Shell who used to preach. One Sabbath, while exhorting the poor, impenitent, hard-hearted, ungrateful slaves, so much beloved by their masters, to repentance and prayerfulness, while entreating them to lead good lives, that they might escape the wrath (of the lash) to come, some of his crocodile tears overflowed his cheek, which so affected his hearers, that they shouted and gave thanks to God, that Brother Shell had at length felt the spirit of the Lord in his heart; and many went away rejoicing that a heart of stone had become softened. But, my readers, Monday morning Brother Shell was afflicted with his old malady, hardness of heart, so that he was obliged to catch one of the sisters by the throat, and give her a terrible flogging.

The like of this is the preaching, and these are the men that spread the Gospel among the slaves. Ah! such a Gospel had better be buried in oblivion, for it makes more heathens than Christians. Such preachers ought to be forbidden by the laws of the land ever to mock again at the blessed religion of Jesus, which was sent as a light to the world.

Another Sunday, when Shell was expounding (very much engaged was he in his own attempts to enlighten his hearers), their was one Jem Fulcrum became so enlightened that he fell from his seat quite a distance to the floor. Brother Shell thought he had preached unusually well so to affect Jem; so he stopped in the midst of his sermon, and asked, "Is that poor Jemmy? poor fellow!" But, my readers, he did not know the secret—*brother Jem had fallen asleep. Poor* Shell did not do so much good as he thought he had, so Monday morning he gave Jem enough of his raw-hide spirit to last him all the week; at least, till the next Sabbath, when he could have an opportunity to preach to him.

I could only think, when Shell took so much glory to himself for the effect of his preaching upon the slaves, of the man who owned colored Pompey. This slaveholder was a great fighter (as most of them are), and had prepared himself for the contest with great care, and wished to know how he looked; so he said, "Pompey, how do I look?" "Oh, massa, *mighty!*" "What do you mean by 'mighty', Pompey?" "Why, massa, you look noble." "What do you mean by 'noble'?" "Why, sar, you look just like one *lion.*" "Why, Pompey, where have you ever seen a lion?" "I seen one down in yonder field the other day, massa." "Pompey, you foolish fellow, that was a *jackass.*" "Was it, massa? Well, you look just like him."

This may seem very simple to my readers, but surely, nothing more noble than a jackass, without his simplicity and innocence, can that man be, who will rise up as an advocate of this system of wrong. He who trains his dogs to hunt foxes, and enjoys the hunt or the horse-race on the Sabbath, who teaches his bloodhounds to follow upon the track of the freedom-loving Negro, is not more guilty or immoral than he who stands in a northern pulpit, and hunts down the flying fugitive, or urges his hearers to bind the yoke again upon the neck of the escaped bondman. He who will lisp one word in favor of a system which will send blood-bounds through the forests of Virginia, the Carolinas, Georgia, Kentucky, and all the South, chasing human beings (who are seeking the inalienable rights of all men, "life, liberty, and the pursuit of happiness,") possesses no heart; and that minister of religion who will do it is unworthy his trust, knows not what the Gospel teaches, and had better turn to the heathen for a religion to guide him nearer the right; for the heathen in their blindness have some regard for the rights of others, and seldom will they invade the honor and virtue of their neighbors, or cause them to be torn in pieces by infuriated beasts.

Mr. James L. Goltney was a Baptist preacher, and was employed by Mr. M. B. Harrison to give religious instruction to his slaves. He often used the common text: "Servants, obey your masters." He would try to make it appear that he knew what the slaves were thinking of—telling them they thought they had a right to be free, but he could tell them better—referring them to some passages of

Scripture. "It is the devil," he would say, "who tells you to try and be free." And again he bid them be patient at work, warning them that it would be his duty to whip them, if they appeared dissatisfied—which would be pleasing to God! "If you run away, you will be turned out of God's church, until you repent, return, and ask God and your master's pardon." In this way he would continue to preach his slave-holding gospel.

This same Goltney used to administer the Lord's Supper to the slaves. After such preaching, let no one say that the slaves have the Gospel of Jesus preached to them.

One of the Baptist ministers was named B. Harrison. He owned slaves, and was very cruel to them. He came to an untimely end. While he was riding out one afternoon, the report of a gun was heard, and he was found dead—his brains being blown out. It could never be found who killed him, and so he went to judgment, with all his sins on his head.

Mr. L. Hanner was a Christian preacher, selecting texts like the following: "The Spirit of the Lord is upon me, because he hath anointed me to preach deliverance to the captives, he hath sent me to bind up the broken-hearted." But Hanner was soon mobbed out of Prince George County, and had to flee for his life, and all for preaching a true Gospel to colored people.

I did not know of any other denomination where I lived in Virginia, than the Baptists and Presbyterians. Most of the colored people, and many of the poorer class of whites, were Baptists.

SABBATH AND RELIGIOUS MEETINGS.

On the Sabbath, after doing their morning work, and breakfast over (such as it was), that portion of the slaves who belong to the church ask of the overseer permission to attend meeting. If he is in the mood to grant their request, he writes them a pass, as follows:—

"Permit the bearer to pass and repass to — —, this evening, unmolested."

Should a pass not be granted, the slave lies down, and sleeps for the day—the only way to drown his sorrow and disappointment.

Others of the slaves, who do not belong to the church, spend their Sabbath in playing with marbles, and other games, for each other's food, etc.

Some occupy the time in dancing to the music of a banjo, made out of a large gourd. This is continued till the after part of the day, when they separate, and gather wood for their log-cabin fires the ensuing week.

Not being allowed to hold meetings on the plantation, the slaves assemble in the swamps, out of reach of the patrols. They have an understanding among themselves as to the time and place of getting together. This is often done by the first one arriving breaking boughs from the trees, and bending them in the direction of the selected spot. Arrangements are then made for conducting the exercises. They first ask each other how they feel, the state of their minds, etc. The male members then select a certain space, in separate groups, for their division of the meeting. Preaching in order, by the brethren; then praying and singing all round, until they generally feel quite happy. The speaker usually commences by calling himself unworthy, and talks very slowly, until, feeling the spirit, he grows excited, and in a short time, there fall to the ground twenty or thirty men and women under its influence. Enlightened people call it excitement; but I wish the same was felt by everybody, so far as they are sincere.

The slave forgets all his sufferings, except to remind others of the trials during the past week, exclaiming: "Thank God, I shall not live here always!" Then they pass from one to another, shaking hands, and bidding each other farewell, promising, should they meet no more on earth, to strive and meet in heaven, where all is joy, happiness and liberty. As they separate, they sing a parting hymn of praise.

From Slave Cabin to the Pulpit

Sometimes the slaves meet in an old log-cabin, when they find it necessary to keep a watch. If discovered, they escape, if possible; but those who are caught often get whipped. Some are willing to be punished thus for Jesus' sake. Most of the songs used in worship are composed by the slaves themselves, and describe their own sufferings. Thus:

"Oh, that I had a bosom friend,
To tell my secrets to,

One always to depend upon
In everything I do!"

"How I do wander, up and down!
I seem a stranger, quite undone;
None to lend an ear to my complaint,
No one to cheer me, though I faint."

Some of the slaves sing—

"No more rain, no more snow,
No more cowskin on my back!"

Then they change it by singing—
"Glory be to God that rules on high."

In some places, if the slaves are caught praying to God, they are whipped more than if they had committed a great crime. The slaveholders will allow the slave to dance, but do not want them to pray to God. Sometimes, when a slave, on being whipped, calls upon God, he is forbidden to do so, under threat of having his throat cut, or brains blown out. Oh, reader! this seems very hard—that slaves cannot call on their Maker, when the case most needs it. Sometimes the poor slave takes courage to ask his master to let him pray, and is driven away, with the answer, that if discovered praying, his back will pay the bill.

CHAPTER IX.

SEVERING OF FAMILY TIES.

AT one time, Mr. George Harrison employed a vessel to take some of his slaves down the river, as he wished to sell them. The vessel came, and anchored off his farm, as an armed fleet would go to make war upon an enemy's country. While this vessel was steering off the shore, the very waves seemed to speak forth in sorrow and mourning to the dreading slave. Not one word of warning was given them, until the vessel was anchored to receive its living freight. Husbands were thrust on board, leaving their wives behind; wives were torn from the arms which should have protected them, and hurried into that living grave; children were torn shrieking from their parents, never to see them more; tender maidens were dragged from the manly hearts which loved them; the ardent lover was scoffingly compelled to break from the entwining arms of his loved one, and bid a final adieu to all the world held dear to his heart. Oh, ye defenders of slavery! tarry here, place yourselves here, in the situation of these miserable beings! *Pro-slavery men and women!* for one moment only, in imagination, stand surrounded by *your* loved ones, and behold *them*, one by one, torn from your grasp, or you rudely and forcibly carried from them— how, think you, would you bear it? Would you not rejoice if one voice, even, were raised in your behalf? Were your wife, the partner of your bosom, the mother of your babes, thus ruthlessly snatched from you, were your beloved children stolen before your eyes, would you not think it sufficient cause for a nation's wail? Yea, and a nation's interference! What better are you than those poor down-trodden children of humanity? With them, such scenes are constantly transpiring.

Mothers! while fondling your darling babes in your arms, and watching, with the eye of a mother's affection, their little mental dawnings, do you ever think of the poor slave mother, who, with equal affection, looks upon her offspring, yet, with a heart full of agony, prays God to take it to himself, before the evil day comes, when it must be goaded and lashed, and then forbidden every consolation of affection? Oh, think of her, pray for her, toil for her?

Fathers! you who stand before your fellow-men and uphold this hellish institution, while your blooming daughters are before you, look at them, and think!—in your own land are thousands of daughters, as lovely, as much beloved, as yours, whose parents cannot protect them, whose parents cannot say, "My daughter! beware of the tempter's snare! My daughter! fly to these arms for protection! My daughter! pour out your sorrows upon your mother's bosom; into her listening ear tell your tale of wrongs; she will guide, she will comfort you!" No, but they must look tamely on and witness their degradation; they must behold them become the spoiler's prey, and presume not to utter one word in their behalf. Why? They are SLAVES! the property of *free-born American citizens*; and why should we *infringe upon their rights?* Ah, father! could you see your daughter in such a situation and not cry aloud for vengeance? And what better are you than the poor slave, whose only sin is, that his skin is, perhaps, one shade darker than yours—*perhaps not even that?*

Young man! will you defend slavery? Will you cast your vote for a slave-holder? Think before you speak; consider well before you act. Could you have that fair young being you one day hope to call your wife torn from you, and publicly sold to the service of a debauchee? Would you think it too much to call on the laws of the land for redress? Would you think it asking too much to call out the whole military force of the country to the rescue? Ah, no! And could you restrain yourselves, and behold the loved forms of your aged parents reeking with their own blood, drawn forth by one who calls himself their master? Indeed, no! no dungeon deep and loathsome enough for such an one; no gibbet too high to swing him on, as an example to all his kind. And what better are your loved ones than those millions of colored suffering brothers and sisters? Ask no more, "Why meddle with slavery?" As you would receive assistance, give it to others.

The vessel to which I have alluded, anchored by Harrison's estate, was made ready to sail on Sunday, that all might witness her departure. Imagination cannot conceive, nor language describe, those parting scenes. When all were on board, a dead silence reigned. No sound, except the harsh voice of the captain, as he gave his orders, and the coarse jests of the sailors, was heard. Slowly the vessel crept along the shore, like some guilty thing, trying to hide itself from the light of day. Then pealed forth upon the Sabbath air a cry of woe that rent the heavens, and was registered there, "Good-by, my husband!" "Farewell, my wife!" "Good-by, children! we must hope to meet in heaven!" With shouts like these, they gazed upon each other as long as the vessel was in sight. Then, indeed, all was over. "Gone, gone, forever," or "left behind," "going, going, farther and farther from the loved ones," these were the cruel reflections. Some returned to their deserted cabins, not one loved one to meet; some fathers drew around them their little ones, bereft of a mother's love; wives sat and wept alone; children wandered about without parents, or any one to love them. Oh, men with hearts, how can you be unconcerned and careless regarding this curse of your country? Oh, my readers, I wish you could enter into my feelings, or rather, that my feelings might enter into your souls, on this subject! God, in His infinite wisdom, created the Ethiopian race with skins of a darker hue than the European. He did so with an all-wise purpose; but was that purpose that they might be subjects of every outrage from their fellow-men, from generation to generation? Oh, surely not! What crime can it be to be born with a dark skin. Who is responsible? The Creator alone. But who are responsible for the crimes perpetrated against them? The *slave-holder* and his *supporters!*

This scene of separation upon the James River, where all the tenderest ties of the human heart were sundered, was but one among the very many which occur daily. Go with the poor bereaved ones the next morning, as they arise from their disturbed slumbers to commence the day of toil. The sight of the master is gall to their wounded spirits; they look not upon the overseer except with absolute horror; but if they falter, they must feel the lash. Even the little crouching, grieving children, are forbidden to weep for their dear parents. The lash, the curse, are their only consolations, except when they can crawl by themselves, and pour out their woes into the sympathizing ear of Jesus, their great Comforter.

My father was living at the time these slaves of Harrison were sold. He was one of his drivers, so he was not sold with them; but he had two brothers who were, and with a heavy heart he had to witness their departure, without daring to say his soul was his own. Monday, he must return to his disgraceful business of whipping his fellows; but what could he do? He must obey his master, or suffer a worse penalty than he could inflict upon others. Some may say, while sitting comfortably among their dear friends, "We would die before we would be guilty of beating, at the command of another, our own kinsmen, perhaps our own children." Ah! it is easy to suppose and assert what you would do, while you are safe; but *you are not a slave!* Your feelings of generous affection may well take deep root, shoot upward and flourish; they are never harrowed up by the sight of tortures you are unable to prevent, never trodden upon and crushed into the dust. You may boast of your manly courage and your willingness to die; it may be the poor slave-driver would crave the privilege of dying for his loved ones, but would it profit those left behind, so long as the lash and a white overseer remained? No! no! hands without a heart might use it—there would be no escape.

Many say the slave on the southern plantation is the happiest creature alive. They don't know; they don't lift the cover; they don't see them always. I have seen many a white man carry a smiling face to the world, when his heart was aching and cankering in wretchedness; I have heard a merry laugh from a maniac, whose brain had been crazed by mental anguish, but I never supposed he was happy; and I have told you, in another place, how these slaves are prepared by rum for company and spectators.

CHAPTER X.

COLORED DRIVERS.

THE colored overseers are not over the slaves because they wish it, but are so placed against their will. When they first commence to lash the backs of their fellows, they are like soldiers when they first go to the battle-field; they dread and fear the contest, until they hear the roaring of the cannon, and smell the powder, and mark the whizzing ball; then they rush into the battle, forgetful of all human sympathy while in fight. So it is with the slave-drivers. They hear the angry tones of the slave-holder's voice admonishing them that if they refuse to whip, they must take it themselves. After receiving the instructions of their owners, they must forget even their own wives and children, and do all they can for "Master". If they do not do this, they must receive all that would be given the others. In this manner, their hearts and consciences are hardened, and they become educated to whipping, and lose all human feeling.

This is the way the slave-holders take to hide their own wickedness. They say the colored driver is more cruel than the white overseer, and use this as an argument against the poor colored man, to show how cruelly they would treat each other if they had the power. Pardon me, my readers, if I say this is an insult to God; since my own experience teaches me better. Reader, when they say that colored drivers are worse than white, the question may well be asked, Why is this? Is it the fault of the colored people, or is it the fault of the white man? Good sense answers to every thinking mind, and says the poor Negro is not the greatest transgressor here, but the white men are the tyrannical instigators of this wrong.

I have known many instances where slaves were put to death by the overseers, without any notice being taken of it by those who administer the laws. Of course, as the word of a black man is not received against a white, nothing could be effected, even if the murderer were arrested. I will give a few cases that came within my own knowledge. James Lewis was shot down by an overseer, and killed. Dick Never was shot down by Owen Woodcock, and killed. Ham was shot by Bishop, and killed. A woman was shot dead by our overseer Hobbs. Wyatt Lee was shot, but not killed. William Painting was shot.

These, my readers, are facts, which will speak for themselves when the great day of reckoning shall come; and those black-hearted sinners will surely be punished, for no sinners escape finally. If the laws of Virginia and other slave-holding states allow them to go unscathed, the eternal laws of justice and right will not.

CHAPTER XI.

MENTAL CAPACITY OF THE SLAVE.

MUCH is said about the inability of the slaves to learn anything but drudgery; that they are fit for nothing else; that those who have ever shown any intellectual power are of mixed blood, not the pure African. This I deny, and I will prove that the African is capable of the highest culture. As a people, how can they be expected to have enlightened minds, when they are denied every privilege of learning? They never have teachers, books are not within their reach—surely, they would be wonderful beings, if, amid all their hardships and privations, they should show themselves scholars! Their ideas of God, heaven and religion, are very simple and childlike; but they are the conceptions of their own uninstructed minds.

The world sees, in the person of Frederick Douglass, what the son of Ethiopia may become. He had no advantages in his youth, but now, before he is old, his fame as an orator has spread over this land, extended itself across the Atlantic, and carried *him* to the shores of the old world, where his eloquence, intelligence and worth, gained for himself and family a name which will adorn the pages of history long after his voice is hushed in death. Had Douglass been educated in youth, there is not a statesman on this continent who would have stood above him.

Then there is Rev. Samuel R. Ward, an unmixed African, who has made great proficiency in learning. His powers as a public speaker are truly captivating, and so ably does he write and speak, that even his enemies acknowledge him to be a man of uncommon power.

There is, also, Rev. Henry Highland Garnett, a son of the same race. He is a scholar, a gentleman and an orator, as all who have seen and heard him admit.

These men are but few out of many, and they prove to the world that the negro is as capable of high intellectual culture as his Saxon brother.

It must be acknowledged by every historian, that Ethiopia was once the most civilized nation upon earth, and that the enlightened nations of the present day are indebted to her for many of the arts of civilization. The people of that country were the first to work in brass, iron and other metals, and were really the first to invent writing, for they used hieroglyphics to express words and ideas, which no other nation had then done. Let it not be said, then, that the Negro cannot be educated. *Free the slaves*, give them equal opportunities with the whites, and I warrant you, they will not fall short in comparison.

I do protest against this great evil of slavery in this civilized land of America, and solemnly appeal to those having authority in behalf of three millions and a half of my suffering brethren who are held by the galling yoke of bondage, that this great evil may be done away, before the retributions of a God of justice overtake this blackest of sins, and scathe the sinner root and branch.

I appeal to the Christian Church to lift up its voice, that it may be heard from shore to shore in defence of the oppressed.

I appeal to the men of America everywhere to help this cause.

I appeal to the women of America, that they plead for their suffering sisters, toiling and weeping under cruel task-masters in the sunny South.

I appeal to little children, that they remember in their prayers those little colored brothers and sisters who are robbed of their parents, have no homes for their weary little frames, no affection to make life lovely to them, no one to teach them and guide them to the Fountain of all Truth.

I appeal to high Heaven to listen to the heartbreaking cries of the captive Negro, and pray the great Jehovah to soften the hard hearts of the many Pharoahs, that they may let the people go free!

CHAPTER XII.

THE BLOOD OF THE SLAVE.

THE blood of the slave cries unto God from the ground, and it calls loudly for vengeance on his adversaries.

The blood of the slave cries unto God from the rice swamps.

The blood of the slave cries unto God from the cotton plantations.

The blood of the slave cries unto God from the tobacco farms.

The blood of the slave cries unto God from the sugar fields.

The blood of the slave cries unto God from the corn fields.

The blood of the slave cries unto God from the whipping-post.

The blood of the slave cries unto God from the auction-block.

The blood of the slave cries unto God from the gallows.

The blood of the slave cries unto God from the hunting-dogs that run down the poor fugitive.

The blood of men, women and babes cries unto God from Texas to Maine. Wherever the Fugitive Slave Law reaches, the voice of its victims is heard.

The mighty God, the great Jehovah, speaks to the consciences of men, and says, "LET MY PEOPLE GO FREE!" And the slave-holder answers, "Who is Jehovah, that I should obey him?" Then the Anti-Slavery voice is heard, calling, "Awake! *Awake!* and cry aloud against this great evil; lift up your voice like a trumpet, and show the people their sins, and the nation its guilt. Pray that God may have mercy upon us. Oh, forgive us this great evil—the evil of selling, whipping, and killing men, women and children! Oh, God of justice! give us hearts and consciences to feel the deep sorrow of this great evil that we have so long indulged in! Lo! we have sinned against Heaven; we have sinned against light—against the civilized world. We have sinned against that declaration which our fathers put forth to the world, *'All men were created equal.'* Oh, God! forgive us this great sin! Oh, let this prayer be heard!"

"WHERE IS THY BROTHER?"

BY MRS. E. L. FOLLEN.

"What mean ye, that ye bruise and bind
My people?" saith the Lord;
"And starve your craving brother's mind,
Who asks to hear my word?

"What mean ye, that ye make them toil
Through long and hopeless years;
And shed, like rain, upon your soil,
Their blood and bitter tears?

"What mean ye, that ye dare to rend
The tender mother's heart?
Brother from sister, friend from friend,
How dare ye bid them part?

"What mean ye, when God's bounteous hand
To you so much has given,
That from the slave that tills your land,
Ye keep both earth and heaven?"

When, at the Judgment, God shall call,
"Where is thy brother?"—say!
What mean ye to the Judge of all
To answer, on that day?

CPSIA information can be obtained
at www.ICGtesting.com
Printed in the USA
BVHW080123100921
616332BV00007B/1176